Eric Ashby

ADAPTING
UNIVERSITIES
TO A
TECHNOLOGICAL
SOCIETY

Jossey-Bass Publishers
San Francisco · Washington · London · 1974

ADAPTING UNIVERSITIES TO A TECHNOLOGICAL SOCIETY
by Eric Ashby

Copyright © 1974 by: Jossey-Bass, Inc., Publishers
615 Montgomery Street
San Francisco, California 94111
&
Jossey-Bass Limited
3 Henrietta Street
London WC2E 8LU

Library of Congress Catalogue Card Number LC 73-22555

International Standard Book Number ISBN 0-87589-222-1

Manufactured in the United States of America

JACKET DESIGN BY WILLI BAUM

FIRST EDITION

Code 7415

The Jossey-Bass

Series in Higher Education

To Edward Shils
for encouragement, criticism, and friendship

※※※※※※※※※※※※※※※※※※※※※※※※※※※※※※※※※※※

Preface

We in the Western industrial nations are at the outset of an unprecedented crisis. The institutions of society are not adapting themselves fast enough to the consequences of technological change; and what does not adapt does not survive. The situation has generated a whole literature of alarm; some of it is sensational and oratorical; some of it claims crediblity because the prophecies are stated not by man but by computer.

The crisis is unprecedented for three reasons. First, similar threats of crisis in the past were evaded rather than confronted. When food ran out, there was virgin soil to be cultivated. When life became intolerable in one country, people immigrated to another. When there was a need for raw materials, the aggressive nations exploited primitive peoples and their natural resources.

Second, there was a buoyant philosophy of progress in the past; every challenge to the welfare of mankind evoked a successful response from technology: the threat of plague succumbed to public health measures, agricultural science multiplied harvests, engineering science and the techniques of mass production brought ordinary working men comforts and amenities which, only a few generations before, would have been the envy of kings. By *progress* people meant continued economic growth resulting in a rising standard of living; and by *standard of living* they meant health, education, material comfort, and above all a great variety of consumer goods available to ordinary people. During the first half of this century, despite two world wars, this optimistic philosophy seemed justified. In affluent nations health improved, access to education became a common right, and a janitor, street-cleaner, or stenographer could drive an automibile to work and go home to central heating, a dishwasher, and colour television. One problem remained: how to spread this high standard of living to the underpriviliged minorities in affluent countries and to the great majority of the world population in the so-called developing countries. Today, however, this happy assumption seems unjustified. The prospect of perpetual economic growth spreading benefits over all people on earth has become a mirage. The gap between haves and have-nots widens. Even those who still have faith in material progress admit that increase in economic growth and innovations in technology essential to progress may not lead to betterment of the human condition but rather to decay.

The third reason why the present crisis is unprecedented is a matter of simple arithmetic. I say "simple" because it is the reenactment of a story told to children for centuries: the request to a king that he give his modest supplicant two grains of wheat for the first square on the chessboard, four for the second, eight for the third, and so on. The king, innocent of the treacherous nature of geometrical progression, did not realize that all the wheat in his kingdom would not suffice to grant the request. The subtlety of growth by geometrical progression or compound interest is that sooner or later a doubling increases the size or number to a fantastic or catastrophic level. It is said that half the scientists who ever lived are alive today, for scientists have been increasing at compound interest. If they continue to increase at the present rate for several doublings their number would become both fantastic and catastrophic; there would not be enough room on earth for all the papers they would write.

Increase by compound interest does not continue indefinitely. It levels off because of constraints upon growth. For the first time on a world scale these constraints are about to come into play. It is a reasonable assumption that world population has increased at compound interest—with periodic local setbacks caused by famine, disease, and war—since man appeared on the earth. But people living now may experience the last doubling of population: it is difficult to believe that the world could carry the consequences of even two or three more doublings at the present rate. We do not know how the levelling off will occur: through stringent birth control, disease, famine, or war. Growth rates in other areas, such as enrolments in higher education and the consumption of energy, have been increasing at compound interest without constraint, too, and will probably level off before the end of this century.

The present problems in industrial countries are unprecedented because they require adaptation to the levelling off of many social activities. We have to devise a life style suited to a steady-state world.

These problems of industrial countries are complicated by two other, quite different, problems. One is that we cannot expect two-thirds of the world population who are still have-nots to sympathise with our predicament or to cooperate in our efforts to resolve it. They still want their share of resources before agreeing to a voluntary curb on consumption. Even birth control is unacceptable to many because children are a source of family income. A second and quite different complication is that technological change increases the order of magnitude of events so that the pressure upon our present values becomes intolerable. Within the lifetime of a man of seventy, for example, the audience one could address has risen from a few thousand to hundreds of millions; the speed and range of travel has changed from a leisurely circumnavigation of the earth by sea to several circuits of the earth a day by rocket; and calculations which would have taken years to do are now done in seconds by computers. These and other recent advances in technology are having unpredicted and alarming second-order effects. Value changes in society are now essential. There is some sign of value changes among the young (mixed up with all sorts of ephemera) but no sign that they are being adequately adopted by society at large.

There are fragile hopes that when disaster seems imminent, the values of society do change. The test-ban treaty between the United States and the Soviet Union is indicative; and the dramatic diminution in radioactive fallout since that treaty is a visible reward for mankind. But if the transformation from growth to stability is to be planned, then value changes must anticipate the threat of disaster. The only social instrument able to achieve value changes in advance is education in the widest sense, which includes the mass media and, in communist nations, the manipulated organs of state propaganda.

Educational institutions are doubly involved in the impending world crisis. On one hand they are the producers of skilled manpower upon which economic growth and technological adaptation depend, and thus the pressure for expansion acts upon them as it does upon other inputs into the economy. On the other hand it is in the shelter of educational institutions that reflection about the future and innovations with respect to values can take place, disengaged from the politics of expediency. This double involvement produces ironic contrasts. For example enrolment in higher education in the United States doubled about every fifteen years between 1870 and 1970, and those who make the blueprints for American higher education aim for universal access to it by the year 2000, at a cost of about 3 percent of the American gross national product. At the same time, in the universities of the United States there is a crisis of confidence in technology as the benefactor of mankind. Criticism is widespread against the consumer society and against preparing students to serve that society. Americans have to accept, therefore, that some of the products of these universities will not promote economic growth or raise material standards of living: they will be counterproductive to these values.

It is not surprising, therefore, that universities all over the world are once more (after long stretches of time when they were no more than trivial appendages of society) institutions of seminal importance, as European universities were in the Middle Ages. Their ascendancy, however, is proving to be uncomfortable. During the

1960s from Berkeley to Tokyo, from Toronto to Sydney, universities felt a tremor in the social foundations on which they are built. Although they tried hurriedly to adapt themselves to these changes in society as they saw them, their adaptations are probably mere short-term expedients; more profound alterations will be needed as affluent nations begin to realise the choices which lie ahead in the transformation from a philosophy of never-ending growth to one of a steady state. Throughout the world there are signs of consistent trends of thought about the new part universities must play in this present phase of their ascendancy.

It is, I suppose, for this reason that several people have asked me to bring together some of my thoughts on the responsibility of universities from pieces written over the past twelve years while I have been deeply involved in discussions and decisions about the future of higher education in Britain. It is too early to write the history of this important and incomplete episode in the life of universities. But it is not too early to assemble some of the documents which may be relevant to this history. This volume puts on record some of the issues which have filled the minds of those of us who chose, during this phase of rapid change, to leave the laboratory for the committee room and administrative office, and to compose agenda and drafts of policy instead of scientific papers.

In a sense this book is a fragment of autobiography: it is a byproduct of an administrator's day-to-day work. Each chapter was written for a specific occasion and only lightly edited for this collection. The first one, on the nineteenth-century idea of a university, was originally given in German as the Queen's Lecture in Berlin in 1967, under the title "Die Zukunft der Universitätsidee des 19 Jahrhunderts." The second chapter, on investment in man, was my presidential address to the annual meeting of the British Association for the Advancement of Science in 1963.

Chapter Three, which discusses some of the potentials and perils of educational technology, was the Joseph Wunsch Lecture, given at the Israel Institute of Technology in Haifa in 1966. Chapter Four, on the relation of government to higher education, originated as the Foundation Oration at Birkbeck College in the University of London in 1968. Chapter Five, about the role of students in academic government, was one of the annual orations at the London

School of Economics; it was written in 1964, when effective participation by students and their concern with college business were still in a rudimentary stage.

Chapter Six, on the academic profession, is based on a lecture given to the British Academy, endowed by the Thank-Offering to Britain Fund, which is a moving tribute by European intellectuals (largely Jewish) who found refuge in Britain from Nazi antiintellectualism and repression. Chapter Seven also originated as a memorial, this time to a great physicist, Arthur Compton, who undertook the arduous duty of becoming a university president at Washington University in St. Louis. It is an attempt to describe—or perhaps I should say circumscribe—the role of the university president.

Chapters Eight and Nine stem from the vigorous debate in Britain about the social responsibilities of scientists and the application of science and technology to human problems. Chapter Eight, "Science and Antiscience," on the scientist's conscience over higher education, was the first of what will be a biennial lecture to the Royal Society on some aspect of the social function of science. Chapter Nine, originally titled "A Balance Sheet for Science and Technology in Europe," stemmed from the Western European Union, which arose out of the Brussels Treaty, signed in 1948. Among the aspirations for European cooperation from this Union was the desire to bring together the universities of Europe. As a step toward this end, a conference of the heads of European and British universities was held in Cambridge in 1955, where Gilbert Murray, a classical scholar of great international reputation, gave the oration. Four years later the heads of the European universities met again, this time at Dijon. I was invited to give the second oration and to take as my topic science and technology in Europe.

Chapter Ten, on the implications of mass education for the structure of higher education, originated as an address to the Second International Conference on Higher Education at the University of Lancaster in 1972.

The raw material which went into the following chapters is thus drawn from British and European experience, but the themes are common to universities everywhere. They include the place of science and technology in higher education; interrelations among the trinity of academic organization—students, teachers, and administrators; the relation of universities and the state; the heritage universities preserve from the past; and the social responsibilities which universities and academics are now expected to discharge.

The debate on these issues has from time to time deviated from the traditions of discourse among scholars and scientists; it has sometimes been coloured by political commitments or surges of emotion. Thus, objective and cool discussion of these problems is likely to be written off as stale liberalism. Nevertheless there must be objective and cool discussion; I offer this book without apology for its low key.

Acknowledgements

The chapters in this book are adapted from lectures, some of which have appeared in print as pamphlets or in journals. For permission to reproduce this material I am indebted to the editor of Minerva (for Chapter One), the British Association for the Advancement of Science (for Chapter Two), the Technion, Haifa (for Chapter Three), Birkbeck College, University of London (for Chapter Four), The London School of Economics (for Chapter Five), The British Academy (for Chapter Six), Washington University (for Chapter Seven), The Royal Society of London (for Chapter Eight), The International Council for Educational Development (for Chapter Nine), and the Secretariat of the Conference of European Rectors and Vice-Chancellors (for Chapter Ten).

Some of the chapters are by-products of studies in the history of higher education in which Mary Anderson and I have been engaged for the last twelve years. I am very grateful to Dr. Anderson for reading and criticising the whole of the typescript and for helping to put it in a form fit for publication.

Finally I want to record my gratitude to JB Hefferlin of Jossey-Bass for the charming and skillful way in which he edited my text to suit the palate of an American readership.

Clare College   Eric Ashby
Cambridge, England
January 1974

Contents

Adapting Universities to a Technological Society

Chapter I

✿✿✿✿✿✿✿✿✿✿✿✿✿✿✿✿✿✿✿✿✿✿✿✿✿✿✿✿✿✿✿✿✿✿✿✿

Idea of a University

The German academic tradition has deeply influenced universities in the United States, Britain, the Soviet Union, and elsewhere. But in each of these countries social forces have acted to adapt the tradition to national needs. Universities therefore have to strike a balance between an adaptation which is too pliable and an adherence to tradition which is too inflexible. To achieve this balance universities need to initiate and control their adaptation to society, not to allow it to be imposed on them from outside.

1

The university is a mechanism for the inheritance of the Western style of civilization. It preserves, transmits, and enriches learning; and it evolves as animals and plants do. Therefore one can say that the pattern of any particular university is a result of heredity and environment.

Let us carry this biological analogy one step further. Among communities of organisms, and among communities of universities, there are episodes of innovation and hybridisation when new forms appear. For universities one of these episodes occurred in the nineteenth century. It was due largely to Wilhelm von Humboldt. The two hundredth anniversary of his birth fell on 22 June 1967. Not only Germany, but the whole world of learning, is in his debt.

There had already been a reawakening of universities in Germany during the eighteenth century; but the moment of destiny for German higher education was 1810, when Humboldt founded a university in Berlin dedicated to a fresh concept of humanism. In the following generations there were, of course, tensions in ideology: a severe intellectualism displaced the humanism of Humboldt and the idealism of Johann Gottlieb Fichte. From time to time the autonomy of the German universities was infringed upon, but nevertheless they became the envy of the Western world. Scholars returned to England and America from Berlin and Göttingen enchanted and eager to reform their own institutions of higher education. To pursue learning was to embark upon an adventure. In Justus Liebig's laboratory in Giessen, for example, students came to work from all over Europe. Every student had to find his own way for himself. Liebig and his disciples were in the laboratory from dawn until far into the night. There were no recreations or pleasures outside the institute. The only complaints came from the attendant who could not get the workers out of the laboratory in the evenings so that he could clean. This would be a familiar experience today, but it was an exciting innovation in 1839.

In that year a student from Britain, Lyon Playfair, came to work at Giessen. Although Liebig welcomed him, he pitted him against one of his own assistants to make an analysis of an unknown substance. The results of the two analyses were identical to the first decimal place. Playfair was accepted as a coworker. It was he, more than any other man at that time, who brought the German style of

academic life to England. Many similar stories can be told about
American students in Germany. Henry P. Tappan, who laid the
foundation of the University of Michigan, Charles W. Eliot of Harvard, Andrew Dickson White of Cornell, Daniel Coit Gilman of
Johns Hopkins: all these men drank from the springs of German
academic life.

From the 1860s until 1914 thousands of young men from
England and America made the pilgrimage to German universities.
An estimated nine thousand Americans studied in Germany during
the nineteenth century, and the number of Englishmen there must
have been at least as large. I recollect my own professor in London
telling us proudly that he had been a pupil of the famous botanist
Julian von Sachs in Würzburg. We felt the continuity of a line of descent, almost spiritual: an apostolic succession of learning. In the German tradition this loyalty of discipleship corresponds to loyalty to a
college in Cambridge and to *alma mater* in Yale. It is no accident that
the *Festschrift* is a German invention.

A new thread of inheritance was woven into the higher education of England and America during the second half of the
nineteenth century. It was the thread of education through training
in science and scholarship (*Erziehung durch Wissenschaft*). Its first
impact was on newly created institutions: University College London,
Owens College in Manchester, the University of Michigan in Ann
Arbor, and Johns Hopkins University, which at its foundation in
1876 had so many German-trained professors it was nicknamed
"Göttingen in Baltimore."

When a gene enters a new environment the manifestation of
that gene may change. This is what happened to German concepts
of a university when they crossed the Channel. Confronted with a
different academic tradition in a different society, the German concepts were assimilated but transformed. There were many reasons
for the transformation. One important reason was that there was no
effective competition among British universities, such as existed
among the universities in the German states. In Germany rivalry
stimulated universities to adopt new ideas. In England higher education was dominated by the influence of Oxford and Cambridge;
prestige was concentrated in these two centres in a way it has never
been in the universities of Germany. Although the new institutions

of higher education in England were in part a protest against the exclusiveness of Oxford and Cambridge, they nevertheless had to live under the hegemony of these ancient universities. They acquired by a process of social mimicry some of the prevailing assumptions about higher education. Prominent among these assumptions in Oxford and Cambridge was a conviction that the university exists to produce servants for church and state,—cultivated men but not intellectuals. It was more important for university graduates to be civilised than learned; they were to be doers not thinkers, bishops not theologians, statesmen not philosophers, schoolmasters not scholars. Liberal education (*Bildung*) rather than vocational training (*Ausbildung*) was the responsibility of the university. This then was the pattern of teaching through the first half of the nineteenth century in an Oxford college: a single tutor nurtured a select group of pupils for three years, and he taught them the whole range of the curriculum. His personality and outlook on life were as much a part of the curriculum as were the Latin texts and Greek philosophy.

It is not surprising that the universities which set the fashion for British higher education stubbornly resisted the idea of research as an instrument of education. As some witnesses told a Royal Commission in 1852, research would propagate infidelity and scepticism. Stimulated by their own reformers Oxford and Cambridge finally accepted the idea (already adopted in the newer universities of London and Manchester) that teaching should be in the hands of professors rather than tutors. However, the underlying purpose of the German university—no longer Humboldt's humanism, but the empiricism of Hermann von Helmholtz—was never fully accepted by British universities. The implicit purpose of British universities was still to make men cultivated, not learned. As Mark Pattison, one of the Oxford reformers, said: the fruit of learning is "not a book, but a man."

To this day the heart of teaching in Oxford and Cambridge (and among many other British universities) is personal confrontation with a tutor; values and style of thinking still count more than facts. The German philosopher and educational reformer Max Scheler (1925) echoed this attitude when he wrote about general education *(Bildungswissen)*.

The matter as well as the manner of teaching is prescribed.

Courses must be studied in a strict sequence, and in most universities examinations must be passed in one course before a student is permitted to proceed to the next. This introduces another element in the German idea of a university which failed to take root in Britain: the freedom of the research worker or student to learn what and how he wishes *(Lernfreiheit)*. The colleges of Oxford and Cambridge regarded themselves as parent substitutes. To be parent substitutes is to restrict freedom of learning. First, a student who has the equivalent of an *Abitur* does not have any right to a place in a university. The university can select and reject whom it likes. Second, an English student finds that once he has chosen the subject he will study, the curriculum he follows, the number of years he takes to complete the course, the intervals at which he is obliged to sit for examinations are all prescribed for him, and he has very little freedom to vary them. Humboldt's vision of solitude and freedom *(Einsamkeit und Freiheit)* for students has never been accepted in the English university.

The freedom of teaching *(Lehrfreiheit)* was eagerly accepted in Britain. It was not only accepted but extended beyond the classroom to cover the "right" of a university teacher to make public assertions beyond his expertise without fear of reprisal. British professors can and do criticise public policy with a degree of freedom which would certainly be denied British civil servants. The reason for this is simple: British universities were never organs of the state. They were and still are autonomous corporations, and university teachers are not civil servants. Freedom of teaching covers the operations of the entire institution and not just the operations of teaching and writing. This expansion of freedom of teaching gives birth to several interesting conventions. For example, 80 percent of the income of British universities is derived from central or local government; yet a convention long ago established that university expenditure was exempt from scrutiny by parliament (although this is now eroded) or by local government.

While all this was happening the German idea of a university crossed the Atlantic. It entered a different environment and underwent different modifications. The most powerful environmental factor in America was not the hegemony of established universities; it was the utilitarian attitude toward higher education. This attitude could be expected from a pioneer and frontier population. It was a reaction against the conservative curriculum which most of the older colleges had inherited from Europe. Even as recently as 1875 the only fulltime studies offered in the first four semesters at Yale University were Greek, Latin, and mathematics. It is no wonder that the German enthusiasm for science in the curriculum and the scholar's dedication to science and scholarship *(Wissenschaft)* were eagerly accepted. But the exuberant interpreters of *Wissenschaft* extended it to subjects of study which no German university would have tolerated. There arose a bewildering variety of offerings. Cornell University, for example, offers about 12,500 courses of study ranging from hotel management to symbolic logic. Students have a wide freedom of choice among these courses. They are awarded degrees after they have accumulated so many credits for attending courses and passing examinations; and within limits the credits can be transferred from one university to another. Clearly some features of the German concept of freedom of learning took root in America although not in Britain. In America, however, there remains a tyranny of frequent examinations which no German university would tolerate.

The German influence worked deeply into American higher education, but it did not produce facsimiles of German universities. Under the influence of American society it produced a new species of university. There is an obvious family likeness. There is a considerable degree of freedom of learning and (apart from some deplorable lapses) as much freedom of teaching as is found in Germany or in Britain. American graduate schools correspond to German institutes. The German prescriptions of unity of research and teaching *(Einheit von Forschung und Lehre)* and education through scholarship receive in the graduate schools an almost ritualistic devotion. But there are two fundamental differences between the American and the German university. First, higher education is a consumer commodity in America, and in an egalitarian society there must be enough of it available for all who want it. Second, there is no minimum common level of achievement for degrees among American universities, such as is guaranteed by the *Staatsexamen* in Germany, the *licence* in France, and the degree examinations conducted by external examiners in Britain. Nor can standards be controlled by a severe selection of students. Consequently there is in America something unfamiliar in the university systems of Europe: a great diversity in quality of education and in the standards of achievement required for a bachelor degree. At first this seems to be a weakness in the system, but in the long run it turns out to be a valuable adaptation to the American environment. Not all qualifications are on the gold standard of learning, but there is a legitimate market for cheap diplomas, as there is for cheap automobiles. This market does not in any way debase the quality of the good institution. Indeed, by siphoning off students with modest aspirations into universities with modest standards, this system protects high standards in the universities which do have international standing. In the bloodstream of American and British universities there is a precious inheritance from the German university, adapted by each country to fit its own academic traditions and style of society.

Turning now from reflection about the past and some of the forces which have determined the pattern of the modern university in America, Britain, and Germany, let us conjecture regarding the future. It is a dangerous future. Today universities everywhere face a common peril: the peril of success. Formerly each was a detached organism, assimilating and growing in accordance with its own internal laws. Now universities have become absolutely essential to the economy and to the very survival of nations. Under the patronage of princes or bishops they were cultivated as garden flowers of no more significance to the economy than the court musician. Under the patronage of modern governments they are cultivated as intensive crops, heavily manured and expected to give a high yield essential to the nourishment of the state. Universities are, then, mechanisms for the inheritance of culture, and like other genetic systems they have great inertia. They are living through one of the classical dilemmas of systems in evolution: they must adapt themselves to the consequence of success or they will be discarded by society: they must do so without shattering their integrity or they will fail in duty to society.

What is the consequence of the success of the universities? Simply, forces from outside the university, which formerly had only a marginal effect upon the evolution of the university, are now likely to exert a powerful influence on this evolution. Governments which hitherto have been content to leave universities alone are now tempted to exert more and more control. Querulous protestations about this are useless. Universities are now very expensive to run. None of them can hope to survive without patrons. Between universities and patrons there have always been buffers of convention. The patron is now the man in the street; universities must negotiate with him and establish new conventions to safeguard what they have inherited. Conventions differ from one nation to another, but the topics of confrontation between universities and society are similar everywhere. Two of these topics are: How large should university systems be? What should universities teach?

The size and shape of a university system are determined by three major forces: the most prominent force in the United States is pressure from students to enter the system; the most prominent force in the Soviet Union is the "suction" (or manpower needs) drawing graduates out of the system; the most prominent force in Germany, and until recently in Britain, is the inner logic of the system itself. In all advanced countries it is now clear that systems of higher education will break down unless there is a balance between these three forces. One thing is certain about the future: the force which I call the inner logic of the university, the heredity of the university, will have to adapt itself to increases in the other two forces coming from the social environment.

In every country there is pressure to increase the size of university systems. The reasons are obvious. If governments finance universities, the children of voters must have a reasonable chance to be placed in them; and since the operations of commerce, industry, and government now depend on technology, the institutions which transmit technology must be expanded to meet national needs.

The patterns of response to this pressure differ considerably from country to country. In Britain the policy is to maintain very good conditions for university education by rigorously restricting the number of students who enjoy these conditions, not by erecting a financial barrier (nine out of ten students in British universities receive financial help) but by a severe number quota based on merit as measured by examinations. One consequence of the British system is that the ratio of output to input is very high. Of every hundred students who enter British universities about eighty-seven earn bachelor degrees; furthermore they do so in the minimum time or at most one year over the minimum time. Those who are not expected to be able to run the course at the prescribed speed are not permitted to enter the race, but they do have the opportunity to continue their training through polytechnics and other colleges of further education. There is a vigorous argument in Britain about how much of this vocational training should carry the promise of a degree, which has (unfortunately) become in Britain a ticket for social mobility. Until this argument is settled the British universities will not adapt themselves to the social forces which are enlarging the university system. The disequilibrium lies not in the treatment of those who are accepted in the universities and who have good conditions for study; rather it is in the treatment of those who are qualified technically to enter universities but who are nevertheless excluded.

In the United States the policy is quite different. There is an open door to higher education. The university course is an obstacle race open to all competitors who care to enter it; but—and this is the significant feature—owing to the diversity of standards among universities, the competitors can choose whether to enter difficult races by going to institutions of international standing or to enter easy races by going to institutions of more modest pretensions. America responds to pressures for expansion by expanding freely, but the expanded system is separated into different levels of quality. There are opportunities for fulltime higher education at some level to four out of ten children, but the American system, like the British, is not yet adapted to the contemporary environment. About half the students who enter American universities fail to complete their courses of study; and in the huge state universities there are two unresolved problems. One is how to provide for the coexistence of mediocrity and excellence within one academic society. The other is how to maintain on a campus of thirty thousand students any contact between teachers and students. If the Americans can solve these problems (and they are making great efforts to do so), it will be a valuable contribution to the security of all universities everywhere since these problems are common to the intellectual life of all egalitarian societies.

The Soviet Union responds to pressure upon the capacity of universities in a different way. The policy is to provide a specialized education on a narrow front in a great variety of technical colleges—there are about 650 of them—for 90 percent of the students. Only 10 percent of the students in the Soviet Union go to universities (this is reminiscent of the Flugge Plan put forward in Germany in 1960). There is, therefore, in the Soviet Union a diversity of institutions stratified according to subject, not as in America according to quality. There too, adaptation has a long way to go before it meets the aspirations of the people. One symptom is that only about half the students in the Soviet Union study fulltime; the others must be content with parttime or correspondence courses.

In Germany every qualified student has a right to enrol for higher education; and the *Honnefer Modell* (a scheme which subsidises university education for gifted students) at least lowers the financial barrier which would otherwise exclude some capable students. The problem of adaptation seems to lie inside the universities rather than outside them. On one hand some students take far too long to complete their studies; on the other hand lecture halls and seminars are crowded. There is great difficulty in preserving the tradition of *Wissenschaft* with the present ratio of teachers to students. The seminar class is often as large as a lecture audience. German professors must envy their predecessors in Marburg ninety years ago, when there were sixty-two professors and lecturers for 430 students. The new environment challenges old practices. For centuries students hung around universities for years, putting off the day of examinations; but irreversible changes in society have transformed what used to be a harmless indulgence into what is now a grave problem. The controversial report of the Council for Higher Education (Wissenschaftsrat, 1966) proposes a prescribed four-year programme and an interim examination in an attempt to resolve this problem. Some of the problems discussed in the report have close parallels to those in large American universities. There is a remarkable convergence of opinion between some passages in the report of the Council for Higher Education and the Muscatine Report on the University of California, Berkeley (1966). These two documents were published within a few weeks of each other. It is interesting that the Council for Higher Education in an earlier report (Wissenschaftsrat, 1960) opposed restricted entry to German universities and opposed even entrance examinations. Instead the report favours one element in the American philosophy: expanding the system until it is large enough to take all qualified candidates. Events are moving too fast for this policy, however. Already in medical faculties, and even in the philosophical faculty at Heidelberg, a number quota is imposed.

The pressure from society to enlarge university systems is a comparatively simple phenomenon. Much more controversial are pressures from society upon courses of study in universities. For one thing, society does not know what it wants. Predictions of the numbers of medical doctors, mathematicians, economists, and so on, which the state will require five years ahead, are notoriously unreliable. Even if they were reliable, it is questionable whether anything but propaganda can be used to persuade students to follow one kind of course rather than another. In Britain, for example, we have tried to plan university development on the assumption that two-thirds of the students would study natural science and technology, and one-third would study humanities and the social sciences. In fact, the present ratio is not two to one but one to one.

But to discuss what universities ought to teach in terms of manpower needs is to touch only the fringe of the problem. The core of the problem is the antithesis (although some would deny that it *is* an antithesis) between education (*Bildung*) and vocational training (*Ausbildung*). No doubt society needs citizens with education even more than with vocational training; and there is no doubt that in America and Britain and Germany the universities admit that they are not supplying this need. The spirit of Wilhelm von Humboldt troubles the consciences of us all.

Let us glance at the problem as it occurs in America, Britain, and Germany. The Muscatine Report on the University of California makes an interesting point: America accepted Humboldt's pattern of a university without introducing his pattern for the intermediate school and this is the cause of much discontent with American higher education. There is something to be learnt from American efforts to dispel this discontent. The theme of the famous Harvard University report on general education (1945) was that all Harvard students, whatever their field of specialisation, should become familiar, through formal, examined courses, with a body of knowledge, ideas, and values which constitute the "heritage of

Western civilisation." At the time this report was regarded as the beginning of a new era in American higher education. It turns out to have marked the end of an old era. When Harvard came to review the general education programme twenty years later, it was clear that this particular technique had failed. Attempts to impart a common core of culture led to the shallow swamps of superficiality. A similar fate seems to have befallen the general education which German universities established in the 1950s. The original general education programme at Harvard has now been abandoned and replaced by a pattern of education which obliges the student to spend some of his formal learning time in courses outside his specialism. A really satisfactory way to do this has not yet been discovered. At the worst it can become an intellectual tourism. Just as we are all adopting package products in our domestic life ("instant" coffee, canned pies, inclusive coach tours to Italy), so are we being pressed to adopt "instant knowledge." The campus bookstore of any American university has shelves of "quick-learn" summaries of everything from world history to English literature. Occasionally (as, for example, in the humanities course at Columbia University)' the formal curriculum for general education does give scientists and technologists an understanding of a world of values. But American opinion is now moving away from the survey course as an instrument of general education toward an attitude which has its origin in Germany. It was a German belief that contact with research was itself a liberal education; by watching a professor working on the frontiers of knowledge, a student understood new techniques of thinking. The most recent American approach (and it is similar to the approach in some of the new British universities) is based on two assumptions. The first assumption is that the best way to enlist the enthusiasm of a student is through the specialism he has chosen. If a student wants to be a physicist, he may well be impatient if he is required to spend part of his time on the heritage of Western civilisation. But if physics is made the core of his discipline, he will respond to courses which discuss the impact of physics on history, its social consequences, and its implications for ethics. If a student is convinced that his nonspecialist studies are relevant to his specialist studies, then he will pursue them with enthusiasm. The second assumption is that what a physicist needs to know about history and what a philologist needs to know about biology is a style of thinking, not a repertoire of facts. This style of thinking can be acquired better from a detailed exposition of one fragment of the subject, given by an active research worker, than from a broad survey.

In Britain we are less interested in curriculum reform than the Americans are. There are many reasons for this, but one reason is outstanding: reverence for science never overcame the influence of such Oxford humanists as John Henry Newman, Benjamin Jowett, and Mark Pattison in the nineteenth century. For them the touchstone of a university education was not to teach great truths, but to teach truth in a great way. What was taught, therefore, was less important than how it was taught. As the English philosopher Samuel Alexander put it: "Liberality is a spirit of pursuit, not a choice of subject."

In present-day German universities the tide of influence, which a century ago flowed so strongly across the Channel and the Atlantic, may now be flowing back to Germany. It would indeed be gratifying if American and British universities could repay some of the debt they owe to Humboldt. Several passages in reports of the Council for Higher Education indicate that Germany may be interested in proposals which we have considerable experience with in Britain. For example, the Council has proposed a diminution of freedom of learning, coupled with an increase in the amount of "pastoral" help offered to students in their studies and even in building character (*Persönlichkeitsbildung*). If the proposals are agreed to, freedom would be restricted by a prescribed sequence of courses, a limited time to complete courses, and an obligation to take an interim examination; though the German student would still have more freedom of learning than his British counterpart. I see from press reports, (*Die Welt*, September 19, 1966) that a sample of students, at any rate, approves these proposals. It has long been a cardinal belief in British universities that the most effective instrument for education was the residential college, where students and faculty members meet together in order to cultivate the intellect. That similar ideas are now being discussed in Germany is evident from the memoranda of suggestions from the Council for Higher Education on college residences (Wissenschaftsrat, 1962). The prime function of these proposed residences is educational: to initiate the new student into the adult life of an intellectual; and it is interesting (as an example of academic influences crossing the Channel from west to east) that the suggestions are strongly influenced by English practice. For example, it is suggested that there should be a mixing of senior and junior members, with wardens (*Kollegienleiter*) assisted by subwardens (*Protektoren*) and tutors (research students), living in the houses and having charge of twenty students each. The Council for Higher Education suggests that some teaching through pro-seminars and colloquia to supplement the university lectures, should go on in the college residences. This proposal is close to the traditional system in the Colleges of Oxford and Cambridge, which the German "invasion" of professorial teaching failed to displace a century ago!

The nineteenth-century idea of a university is a hybrid, with a heredity from Germany, Britain, and America. It is a German trait—of course any summary greatly oversimplifies the matter—to put emphasis on the *subject* rather than the *student*. As Humboldt wrote in 1810: (reprinted 1964): "The relationship between teacher and student . . . is changing. The former does not exist for the sake of the latter. They are both at the university for the sake of science and scholarship." So arose the idea of education through training in scientific and scholarly research; so, too, the idea that teaching and research are inseparable. It is an English trait (I am still oversimplifying) to put emphasis on the cultivation of the student's intellectual health. "To discover and to teach," wrote Newman (1915), "are distinct functions"—and he recommended a division of intellectual labour between academies (for research) and universities (for teaching). In Britain we no longer fully agree with Newman, but some of his influence remains: we still regard ourselves as parent substitutes regarding our students' minds, if not regarding their morals. It is an American trait to emphasize that there is no wall separating scholar from citizen or academic knowledge from useful knowledge. The great seal of Cornell University has inscribed upon it these words: "I would found an institution where any person can find instruction in any study."

Many elements in this heredity are now being challenged by the environment. Universities are at a phase of self-examination. American universities confess that they have been weakened through admitting too many students and teaching too many subjects. British universities are finding themselves obliged to review their traditional paternal attitude toward students. In Germany the Council for Higher Education (Wissenschaftsrat, 1962) has written: "The universities can no longer disregard the question whether education through training in scientific and scholarly research is still possible and adequate." The inner logic of universities is under pressure from governments, the public, and students themselves. Yet one thing is certain: at the end of this century society will still need universities. They will not be needed merely to train professional manpower; they will be needed to serve the intellectual needs of our grandchildren. Something, therefore, of the nineteenth-century inheritance must be preserved. Now is the time to assert what must be preserved.

Universities still need freedom, detachment, and opportunity for solitude, adapted to a new age. But they also need something not so necessary in Humboldt's time because now the wave-length of change is shorter than the lifespan of man. They need one reform which, if it could be achieved, would subsume all other reforms: the ability to initiate their own adaptations to society. They are already capable of some self-change, but the resistances are very great. It is a melancholy fact that universities have not devised efficient built-in mechanisms for change. There are, of course, some virtues in inertia, but not if the inertia is so great that change has to be imposed from outside. Such changes are often so violent that they endanger the heredity of the university. Anyone with experience of universities knows that academic evolution, like organic evolution, is accomplished in small continuous changes. Major mutations are generally lethal. Change must be based upon what is already inherited. Through a study of the descent of universities from their medieval ancestors and their effects upon one another in the contemporary world, we might learn how to control their evolution through the rest of this century. No one can predict what Europe will be like at the dawn of the twenty-first century; yet we do know one thing: the men and women who will be in posts of responsibility then are already university students. The future of the nineteenth-century idea of a university is in their hands.

Chapter II

✿✿✿✿✿✿✿✿✿✿✿✿✿✿✿✿✿✿✿✿✿✿✿✿✿✿✿✿✿✿✿✿✿✿✿

Investment in
Man

The university is a social instrument for investment in man. The policies of investment cannot be decided on economic criteria alone, but it is important to apply some principles of cost efficiency to systems of higher education. When this is done, it is found that many improvements can be made. Among these improvements is an improved use of educational technology and a rephasing of higher education so that it is not concentrated in a few years after high school but is dispersed through a person's whole career.

16

Alfred Marshall wrote that the most valuable of all capital is that invested in human beings. This is my theme here. The advancement of science has its roots in the educational process. We have abundant evidence that our present investment in science is restricted by our educational policies over the last generation. One needs only to study the pages of advertised vacancies for scientists and technologists to realise the extent of the restriction. Regarded in its lowest terms, investment in man brings high economic rewards; and, in its highest terms, investment in man is a moral obligation which the state owes to its citizens. In 1858 the Newcastle Commission on the State of Popular Education in England was told: "It is quite possible to teach a child soundly and thoroughly . . . all that is necessary for him to possess in the shape of intellectual attainment, by the time he is ten years old." We now invest more wisely than that in the young people of Britain but still not wisely enough.

Investment in man covers all education from primary school to the training of research workers. Even if we confine ourselves to investment in man for the advancement of science, we are still left with too large a canvas. Science cannot be isolated; it is part of the seamless fabric of civilization. The advancement of science depends not only upon the training of professional scientists; it depends also upon the public image of science, which is a product of the machinery which weaves science into contemporary culture: scientific journalism, science fiction, and communication of ideas about science through radio, film, and television.

Three questions may be discussed in considering investment in man at the level of higher education: What are the resources of ability for this investment in man? What policies and principles guide investment in these human resources? What is the state of our knowledge about the social institutions we use as instruments for this investment?

In 1962 some 113,000 boys and girls in Britain completed a course of secondary education with sufficient success to qualify them for some form of fulltime higher education. They represented only about 14.5 percent of the age group, and of this percentage only about half met the requirements for entering a university. What happened to the rest? Some 26,000 of them embarked on a secondary school course but left before completing the school-leaving examinations; and some 474,000 of them left school before they reached the age of sixteen. The education of early leavers is not necessarily over: through training and apprenticeship programs with day release, and the like, both government and industry continue to invest in many of them. But apart from those few who later on will break away from work to go to college, these young people will not receive any further fulltime education.

What are the available human resources for fulltime higher education? What principles guide our investment policy for these boys and girls? In 1962* about 64,500 of them enrolled for the first time as fulltime students in universities and colleges (about 30,200 in universities, about 15,500 in colleges of technology, schools of art and commerce and similar places, and about 18,800 in teacher-training colleges). This is only about 55 percent of those qualified for higher education, drawn from the already depleted human resources in this age group in Britain. To put these figures in perspective, consider five children born in 1953: an American, a Canadian, an Australian, a Russian, and a British child. There is about one in three chance that the American is now receiving a full time higher education. The equivalent chance for the Canadian is one in six, for the Australian one in nine, for the Russian one in twelve, and for the British child—but only if one includes all those taking sandwich courses—also one in twelve. No one supposes that these ratios represent differences in resources of ability between these countries. What then do they represent? They represent differences in policy for investment in man. These comparative figures are often used to support indignant arguments about the inadequacy of provision for higher education in Britain. They are quite unreliable for this purpose. They omit students who enrol in parttime courses and who are an integral and valuable part of our system; they omit the population of pupils in sixth forms, who are doing work equivalent to first-year university work in Australia, Canada, and the United

* There has been a change in the investment policy described in this and the following paragraphs. More people of college age now have access to higher education in Britain, but the proportion is still much lower than that in the United States and will remain so for the foreseeable future. But see Chapter Ten.

States; and they omit any consideration of failure rates. Thus, some figures were published recently comparing university enrolments in a dozen European countries, together with Canada and the United States. When the data are calculated as enrolments per age group, Britain is eighth on the list out of twelve and comes below such European countries as Belgium, France, Greece, and Sweden. But when the data are calculated as the number of first degrees (per median age of taking a degree) Britain rises to fourth place on the list. There is a simple reason for this: the efficiency of a British university measured by the number of degrees awarded compared with the number of students who enrol in the hope of getting degrees is about 85 percent, whereas the efficiency of most universities abroad is much lower. In Canada the corresponding percentage is 66, in the United States it is somewhere between 50 and 60, and in Australia it is less than 60.

This striking superiority in the efficiency of British universities concerns the policies and principles which guide our investment in human resources. The American system and our own illustrate two fundamentally different approaches to investment in man. The American policy of investing in human resources is to maximise the number put into the machinery. Even so, not all American talent by any means is invested in higher education. It has been estimated that in the 1950s even at the highest level of intelligence—the top 0.1 percent of ability level—only two out of three Americans graduated from college.

In Britain we follow an entirely different policy for investment in man. By the age of twelve the door to fulltime higher education is all but closed to eighty out of one hundred children. The remaining twenty are selected for specialised privileged schooling which brings them to the gates of colleges and universities, but only about eight out of the twenty get in. We rigidly select a small group of young people and sponsor this group through a heavily subsidised education of very high quality under very good conditions.

Our British policy for higher education is tenable only on certain assumptions. The first is that the techniques for selection are efficient, reliable, and satisfy social justice. The second is that the numbers of young people selected each year for higher education are sufficient for the needs of the nation. The third is that we offer acceptable opportunities for parttime further education to those who are not selected for fulltime higher education. None of these assumptions is justified.

Our methods of selection assume that our intellectual resources are limited by genetic factors and that when we select candidates to go to grammar schools or to universities we are drawing from the population with the innate ability to profit from privileged education. The intellectual resources in a population are ultimately limited by its genetic makeup, but inequalities in our society and inadequacies in our educational system, rather than genetics, at present limit our investment in man; and this is true even in the most affluent nations. There is now convincing evidence that thousands of children fall out of our educational system each year not because they lack ability, but because they lack motive, incentive, and opportunity. A child who succeeds in climbing the ladder of education has responded to a challenge. If there is no challenge there can be no response; and our machinery for selection, unlike that in many countries, is in fact a machinery for distributing challenges. The trouble is that we cannot distribute these challenges justly because our selection methods do not simply separate those who are fit to go to college from those who are not fit: they have to pick out, from a cohort of candidates most of whom are fit to go to college, those who are to fill the limited and inadequate number of places. Under these circumstances, following the success or failure of those we select is no adequate test of our methods of selection; we must also follow the success or failure of those we reject. On the one or two occasions when this has been done we find what indeed we might have expected: the majority of those rejected by one university got into another or took degrees externally; and (in such statistical studies as have been made) the chance of academic success among the rejected candidates was no worse than that among the accepted candidates. There is, as one might expect, a general correlation between success in school-leaving examinations and success in degree examinations. This is useful information for statistical purposes, for example for calculations of the potential size of the university population in Britain; but it gives no reliable guide to the decision the admissions officer has to make: shall I admit John Brown or Peter Smith? It is ironic that the one feature of the investment of man in higher education which we have studied scientifically leads merely to the conclusion that we could invest a much larger proportion of the age group than we do. Three facts confirm this view. The first is that in 1952 about twenty thousand freshmen entered British universities to read for first degrees; 80.6 percent of them were successful. Five years later the number of freshmen entering British universities increased by about a third to twenty-seven thousand. Some people even then talked of a dilution of quality among students, about "scraping the bottom of the barrel", but the proportion of this generation of freshmen who successfully graduated did not fall; it rose to 82.8 percent. The second fact is that the combined percentage of "good honours degrees" rose from 18.6 percent in 1952 to 21.4 percent in 1958, although numbers of students graduating over that period also rose by 6 percent. The third fact is that between 1957 and 1962 the number of government studentships awarded for research training in science and technology rose by 85 percent (from 649 to 1194); but the percentage of "good honours degrees" among these new award holders remained exactly the same: 81.7 percent.

We are uneasy in our search for talent. We spend a great deal of time and energy over the problems of selection, and we are tempted to believe that there must be a "right" way to select students for admission to universities if only we could discover it. Of course there is no right way and it is vain to seek one. It is our policy for investment in man which leads us into this Calvinism of the intellect. "Every selection," said the German philosopher Jaspers (1960), "is in some way an injustice. We delude ourselves when we think that we can avoid such injustice through rational and determined effort."

The second assumption, that our system of higher education is on a big enough scale to meet our future needs for scientists and technologists, is untenable in the light of recent studies of manpower requirements. The third assumption, that there are acceptable alternatives for those who are not selected for fulltime higher education, does need comment. There is nothing inherently unsound—indeed there are great merits—in systems of parttime further education integrated with employment. The trouble with these systems in Britain is their inefficiency. We can well be satisfied with a system of university education which, through the use of external examiners, secures a common standard for all first degrees in all British universities and an 85 percent chance that a student will reach this common standard. The worm which gnaws at our satisfaction is that we have worked out a successful solution to this problem of quality control at the expense of a far greater problem which we have shirked: how to invest efficiently in the rest of our resources of talent. While our wastage rate in universities is commendably low, we cannot forget the heavy casualties among young people who do not get fulltime higher education and who try to qualify themselves through night classes, day release, and correspondence courses. The examination statistics for Ordinary National Certificates give the failure rate among these students as 50 percent, and in one London technical college 42 percent of the evening students working for National Certificate dropped out in their first year. The examination statistics for bodies which award professional qualifications in accountancy, surveying, insurance, and the like are equally distressing. Wastage rates such as these are not the fault of the colleges for further education. They do their best to teach well. They are the fault of our social system which denies to the parttime student an opportunity to learn well.

To say that our national policy for higher education is based on untenable assumptions is not to suggest a colossal proliferation of universities in Britain. An indiscriminate inflation of the volume of investment in man would certainly not pay off. We need to know far more than we do about the pattern of higher education which is likely to be relevant to the lives graduates are going to live. If there were more university places in Britain, no doubt there would be an increase in student enrolment and in the number of students who obtain degrees. The problem is whether—given our present curricula, teaching methods, and pattern of degrees—this would be in the best interests of the nation and of the students. We cannot dissociate any increase in the volume of investment in man from change in the pattern of investment.

The university is a social instrument for investing in man. Consider the remarkable ecology of universities. Universities date back to the Middle Ages and they girdle the earth. From the plains of Lombardy they have been transplanted to the gray climates of northern Europe, to the African bush, to American cities. They have invaded the ancient civilisations of Egypt and India and driven out institutions deeply rooted in the indigenous culture. They have adapted themselves to totalitarian and to democratic societies, to rural communities and to urban technologies. But through time and space they have preserved something resembling a genetic identity, they remain unique as instruments for investment in man. I cannot define this identity but I can describe it from its products. At their best, universities endow the men and woman who pass through them with a characteristic intellectual equipment: the capacity to reconcile orthodoxy and dissent. Intellectual life demands a respect for what has gone before and acceptance of a rigorous discipline to a tradition of learning. To this extent universities are a point of stability in society: they anchor a society to its past. But orthodoxy is celibate; it breeds no fresh ideas; unless tradition is continually re-examined, it becomes oppressive. So in the course of their evolution universities have learnt not only to pass on a body of knowledge and ideas but to train students to disclose errors in knowledge and to question ideas. Some words Michael Polanyi (1962) wrote about science can be applied to all the activities of a university: "The professional standard of science must impose a framework of discipline and at the same time encourage rebellion against it . . . This dual function . . . is but the logical outcome of the belief that scientific truth is an aspect of reality and that the orthodoxy of science is taught as a guide that should enable the novice eventually to make his own contacts with this reality . . . The capacity to renew itself by evoking and assimilating opposition to itself appears to be logically inherent in the sources of the authority wielded by scientific orthodoxy."

To train young people in this dialectic between orthodoxy and dissent is the unique contribution which universities make to society. Any change in the pattern of universities which endangers this function endangers the society which the university serves. For this reason universities combine teaching with research, and endeavour to include among their students those who have the combination of temperament and intellect to profit from this particular approach to learning. But universities could not stay in business if they concentrated only on this unique function; indeed this function arises as a byproduct of a bread-and-butter job of training men and women for the professions. It is for their bread-and-butter service that the public is willing to invest money in them and it is on their discharge of this service that their efficiency is judged.

The very word *efficiency* applied to universities is anathema to some academic men. But there is no reason why our instruments for investment in man should be immune from the criteria of efficiency any more than our instruments for government or for the administration of justice are immune. Nor is there any reason why we should regard research into the production of educated people as any less important than research into the production of steel or artificial fibres. But we shy away from the idea of education as a technology. The techniques of education in Britain have scarcely been touched by the scientific revolution. This is particularly true in universities. Although dedicated to the pursuit of knowledge, they are reluctant to pursue knowledge about themselves. Despite the fact that the annual expenditure on universities in Britain runs into scores of millions, expenditure on studying the processes of teaching and learning at university level is negligible. Indeed this distaste for research extends over the whole field of education. Despite recent grants by the Ministry of Education, the work being done by the National Foundation for Educational Research, and the imaginative projects being supported by the Nuffield Foundation, the proportion of expenditure on research in education to the annual expenditure on education in Britain is less than 5 pence per pound sterling. Any industry which devoted so little to research and development would collapse.

Accordingly, when we come to ask whether our universities are appropriate instruments for investment in man, we lack the data to provide an answer. Each question we ask leads us into untested assumptions. To test whether the assumptions are valid, we need to undertake a sustained programme of research on British higher education. Until this research is done the questions remain unanswered.

The prime question concerns the future of the academic profession. Britain is already committed to a large expansion of higher education. There is already widespread criticism that the scale of expansion is far too small. Pressure to get into college is greater than the experts predicted. It is a simple matter to put up buildings to accommodate increased numbers of students, provided the state will pay for them. What we are not so sure about—even if the state does provide money to pay the salaries—is where teachers of the right academic quality are coming from. Even on our present overmodest calculations for the universities alone (and they account for only about half the traffic in higher education) it is estimated that some eight thousand additional teachers will be required over and above replacements. Prophecy is dangerous, and I may well be proved wrong, but in some subjects—especially in mathematics, science, and technology—I fear either a decline in quality of university teachers or a shortage in quantity.

It would seem prudent under these conditions to do some operational research on teaching and learning in universities. A convenient starting point is a phrase frequently heard nowadays: "the burden of teaching." You hear this more commonly than you hear doctors refer to the burden of healing or lawyers to the burden of litigation. The burden of teaching is measured by a mystic number called the staff-student ratio, which has its origin in the Talmud. Two millennia ago the Rabbi Baba established the rule: "Twenty-five students are to be enrolled in one class. If there are from twenty-five to forty an assistant must be obtained. Above forty, two teachers are to be engaged." One might have thought that with the advent of printing, the film, closed-circuit television, and the tape recorder this ratio would have diminished. But in British universities it has increased to about one teacher per ten students—a higher ratio than is to be found in any other European universities or in most colleges in the United States. It is taboo in the academic profession to contemplate any diminution in this ratio. It must be emphasised that the cause of the higher ratio is the smallness of the denominator rather than the largeness of the numerator; it is another consequence of the British policy for investment in man. So, as we change this policy by admitting larger numbers to higher education, we face a dilemma, at any rate in mathematics, science, and technology: is it better to retain at all costs the quality of university teachers, even if it means less teaching per student and an increase in the staff-student ratio? Or is it better at all costs to maintain the present staff-student ratio, even if it means the recruitment of some mediocre teachers, so that as one American university president put it: "The teacher can communicate his mediocrity in an intimate environment"?

The rational way to pursue this question is to anatomise the working day of a university teacher. According to estimates made by the University Grants Committee, nearly half his working time is spent in research. Let us concede straightaway that this time must not be eroded; although a lot of research is trivial and is (I suspect) done for reasons other than an enthusiasm for the advancement of knowledge, yet this is the seedbed for creative work and it must be left undisturbed. The balance of his time is spent in administration and teaching. Good management can always minimise administration. The difficult question is whether the techniques of learning and teaching in universities could be improved. There is evidence that they could. For some years the Fund for the Advancement of Education in the United States has promoted a massive and sustained programme of operational research on teaching and learning in American universities. The results of this research, together with such fragments of work as have been published in Britain, are sufficient to dispel any complacency we may have about the efficacy of our teaching methods, and they make nonsense of any doctrinaire assertions about staff-student ratios.

Research on learning and teaching is notoriously difficult to interpret because students are astonishingly resilient and adaptable creatures. Give them less teaching, and they compensate by working harder on their own. Introduce some novelty, such as teaching by closed-circuit television, and they may respond favourably not because it is a better method of teaching but because it is a novelty. However, when allowance is made for all these sources of error, the results of research indicate beyond doubt certain simple conclusions about university teaching. The first is that for formal lectures large classes are better than small ones, if only for the simple reason that the lecturer takes more trouble to prepare them. As everyone who has to give lectures known perfectly well, if he has to address five hundred people, and especially if his address is to be televised or filmed, he is, as it were, raised to a temperature of excitement which makes for a better performance. Second, as one would expect, the experiments confirm the value of teaching by discussion in small groups. But what size of groups? The amount of teaching to be done is increased fourfold if tutorials are taken in groups of three instead of in groups of twelve. There is no evidence that teaching is always more effective if the groups are very small. Indeed such little evidence as we have indicates that for some subjects a seminar of twelve is more effective than a tutorial of three. Third, students do better in examinations if they are left to work on their own and are not overtaught. This is a truism; three centuries ago Comenius wrote that his object was "to seek and find a method by which the teachers teach less and learners learn more." The novelty is that the methods known to Comenius can now be improved. If students working on their own have access to audio-visual aids, they can cover, at their choice of time and at their pace of working, the more didactic parts of a course with very little formal teaching. Fourth, modern techniques of instruction such as language laboratories, films, taped discussions, and (for certain parts of certain subjects) programmed instruction are useful for some teaching even at university level. These technical devices save the teacher time which he can use more effectively in the intimate encounter of discussion, which no modern technique can replace. Far from dehumanising and mechanising instruction (a charge frequently brought against them) these modern devices allow the individual to work on his own at his own pace: they actually encourage individuality. Programmed instruction, for example, is merely a return to the Socratic method: the student is not passive; he takes part in a dialogue which makes continuous demands upon him and evokes continuous response from the teacher.

The introduction of technology into teaching and learning at university level evokes such emotional reactions that it is difficult to persuade some people to contemplate it objectively. Gadgets cannot replace the teacher when he is engaged in education and not just instruction because in teaching at the highest level there has to be feedback from students to teacher, to which the teaching is constantly adjusting itself. But a good deal even of university teaching is at a lower level than this, and the aim of technology should be to relieve university teachers of didactic instruction. Professors once had to reconcile themselves to the invention of printing, which enabled the solitary student, alone in his room with a book, to confront the great teacher through the printed word. Some teachers protested, just as centuries earlier teachers protested against writing as a substitute for oral tradition. Now after nearly five hundred years without much change in the technology of higher education, professors will undoubtedly have to reconcile themselves to new inventions, which will enable the student to confront the great teacher in a new and vivid way. We witness only the rudimentary stages of this transition. We are at that awkward phase when the techniques follow the old vestigial patterns, just as the first written instruction still retained the form of dialogue and the first printing resembled manuscript written with a quill pen. Under the impact of research into the techniques of teaching and learning, the whole pattern of education is likely to change. Just as the good teacher of today is complementary to the book and the laboratory, so the good teacher of tomorrow will be complementary to the lecture by television, to the voice recorded on tape, and to the scientifically planned programmes for didactic instruction.

The assumptions we make about the teleology of a university —its function—are just as much in need of scrutiny as the assumptions we make about its operation. The most difficult question of all in considering universities as instruments for investment in man is: What do we want our system of higher education to do for the people we put through it?

The chief assumption we make about this question is evident from the pattern of courses in English civic universities. In most of them the great majority of students in arts and science are reading for special or honours degrees. This pattern presupposes one of two assumptions: either these students are going to become professional scientists and scholars; or the training appropriate for an academic is the best training to give students who are not going to become professional scientists and scholars. The second assumption may well be correct, but at present we hold it only as an article of faith; and so it will remain until we know more about the sociology of professional life. The first assumption is easily disproved. In 1959 and 1960, for example, no fewer than 8441 students graduated in one or other of the single honours subjects: history, classics, English, and modern languages. Of these students only 739 (about 8 percent) were reported as going on to research and advanced study. Was this intensive training, largely in a single arts subject, the best way to invest in the other 92 percent of these graduates? In science and technology a larger proportion (about 20 percent) were reported as going on to research and advanced study, and many of the others went into posts where they were required to do scientific work. But again one asks whether the intensive training, especially the long period spent in the laboratory learning practical techniques, was the best way to invest in the 80 percent or so of graduates in science and technology who did not go on to high-level academic research. It is a system we copied from Germany in the 1860s. Whether it is still the best way to invest the time of a British student, we do not know.

We make untested assumptions not only about the pattern of courses, but about their content. Here is one example. All but the most deeply entrenched pedants agree that education should be relevant to society; for this reason medieval students studied theology and renaissance students studied Greek. If we begin to catalogue the characteristics of our own age, we soon find that among the outstanding features of modern life is what Peter Drucker calls the "application of systematic knowledge to work." This activity is now part of our cultural atmosphere, invisible because of familiarity. People engaged in mass communication—from the advertising agent who writes a toothpaste advertisement or who boosts a new car model, to the scientist broadcasting on the causes of lung cancer or the technology of rockets—assume that their words will be more convincing if supported by scientific evidence, graphs, statistics, data. This—much more than household gadgets and transistor radios—is technology diffusing into the common culture. But education has not yet accepted technology as a form of humanism. The idea that there is no point in learning history unless you are going to become an historian would be treated (and rightly so) with contempt. But the idea that there is no point in learning technology unless you are going to become a technologist still seems perfectly natural. In fact this idea is just as deserving of contempt, because already no man can regard himself as adequately educated if he does not understand some of the principles of technology: the art and science of the application of systematic knowledge to work.

There is one more assumption built into our present policy for investment in man which is of critical importance. Education, as one of my colleagues said, "is not an act of salvation, after which one is safe for eternity." Yet we assume it is: in particular, that a three-year undergraduate course is sufficient to set a man up for a lifetime. Doubtless in the nineteenth century a three-year course in classics did set a man up for a lifetime; but that was in the days when a graduate could assume that he would grow old in a world familiar to him as a youth. We are living in the first era for which this assumption is false, and we have not yet faced the consequences of this fact. The present generation of students will still be employed in the year 2000; but long before then their degrees and diplomas— at any rate in science, technology, and the social sciences—will have become obsolete. The only students who can be sure of escaping obsolescence are those very few who will become innovators. Our investment in the rest—the great majority of our human resources— will inevitably be devalued by technological and social change. Measures to combat obsolescence, therefore, become of prime importance.

What measures have already been taken? There is a plentiful supply of scientific and professional journals. But this is not enough: reeducation, like education, requires challenge and response, an encounter between teacher and student. Refresher courses offer this, but the extent to which they are used and the scope and duration of most of them are pitifully inadequate to meet the need. For example, the Ministry of Education and many other bodies arrange short courses for teachers, covering such topics as mathematics, science, and audio-visual aids for the teaching of modern languages. These courses are very valuable but most of them last only for four to seven days. There are some one-year, fulltime courses of advanced study, but in 1961–1962 they were attended by fewer than four hundred teachers. There is no evidence that any educational institution is planning to offer sustained courses of reeducation on a massive enough scale to prevent widespread obsolescence of teachers.

In technology the story is similar. Some universities and colleges put on short courses of reeducation for technologists, but by no stretch of imagination could these courses be regarded as a comprehensive system to prevent obsolescence. In the training of physicists and chemists there is no sign that any provision is to be made. In medicine the University of London has set up the British Post-Graduate Medical Federation to offer courses to general practitioners; but most of these courses are only for weekends or single weeks, and again they cannot meet the need for sustained and systematic reeducation to prevent obsolescence in the medical profession.

We already spend large sums, even if they are inadequate, on higher education in Britain. We shall be asked to spend a great deal more in a massive programme for investment in man. A large proportion of this expenditure will be devoted to science and technology. But this investment in man will inevitably depreciate as the volume of effort in science and technology increases throughout the world. There is need for drastic steps to prevent obsolescence. Here is an opportunity for the extramural departments of our universities (which are, in any case, seeking for a new inspiration), although universities and colleges cannot alone sponsor a programme to combat obsolescence. Cooperation is required from employers to release men on full pay for sustained fulltime courses every few years. Perhaps the time may come when a degree or a professional qualification, like a passport, is valid only for a limited number of years and is renewed only after attendance in a systematic course of reeducation. The task of higher education is to provide a "framework within which continuous innovation, renewal and rebirth can occur" (Gardner, 1961). In the disturbing, stormswept, feverish years remaining to this century, nothing less than this will suffice for investment in man.

Chapter III

✿✿✿✿✿✿✿✿✿✿✿✿✿✿✿✿✿✿✿✿✿✿✿✿✿✿✿✿✿✿✿✿✿✿✿✿✿

Technology in Education

Advances in the technology of education, despite possible dangers, is enabling mass higher education to become a reality. But education in technology and the implications of technological advances is essential if higher education is to deal effectively with reality.

In the long history of education there have been four intellectual revolutions. They occurred among different people at different times. At first (and in some communities this is still true), education was a responsibility of the extended family. Through fables, stories, and initiation ceremonies children were taught the tribal heritage and trained to take their place in society. Then, in one country after another and for a variety of reasons, education became professionalised. Children were assembled together and taught by experts. In Israel this happened on a large scale at the time of the Maccabees, partly as a defense against the infiltration of Hellenistic culture. The prime purpose of the first Jewish schools was to give religious instruction. This, too, was the prime purpose of schools in the Muslim world, in the cathedral schools of Europe, in the monasteries of India, and of the first schools in tropical Africa, set up by Christian missionaries. When part of the responsibility for education passed from the home to the church or synagogue, this was the first revolution.

Another revolution, closely related to the first and in many places preceding it, was the adoption of the written word as a tool of education. The written word was not everywhere willingly accepted; indeed some of our ancestors opposed it as vehemently as some of our colleagues today oppose teaching by television. We have on record the views of Socrates (*The Phaedrus*) about the dangers of written knowledge: "For this invention of yours will produce forgetfulness in the minds of those who learn it, by causing them to neglect their memory, inasmuch as, from their confidence in writing, they will recollect by the external aid of foreign symbols, and not by the internal use of their own faculties." He also objected to written work on other grounds: "And so it is with written discourses. You could fancy they speak as though they were possessed of sense, but if you wish to understand something they say, and question them about it, you find them ever repeating but one and the selfsame story."

Socrates' objection was that the written word cannot engage in dialectic; and dialectic, together with grammar and rhetoric, were for the Greeks the instruments of teaching. The tutorial system, which originated in Greece, relied on oral tradition; and it is interesting that the literary form of much early writing was dialogue. Similar objection to the use of written material in education is reported from the early Indic civilisation (Myers, 1960). In the reign of Asoka writing was widely used for administrative purposes, but it was rejected for the transmission of sacred literature: passages from the sacred books had to be communicated by mouth and learnt by heart, not read.

The third revolution was the invention of printing. Just as early written material took the form of dialogue, so early printing had the appearance of script. (A modern analogy which can be seen in museums is the way early automobiles were designed, even to the headlamps, to look like horse-coaches). As with the written word, the use of printing to disseminate literature was not everywhere adopted without opposition (Myers, 1960). It is said that a press set up in Constantinople in the eighteenth century generated such fierce opposition from the Muslims that it had to be abandoned, and "no book was printed in Muslim lands until the year 1825, when a press was set up in Cairo" (Carter, 1931).

We are now confronted by a fourth revolution in education. During this century, for the first time since the invention of printing, new technologies are being adopted in teaching which will certainly transform the whole process of education, though what the transformation will be is still a matter for speculation. The technologies are already familiar: film and gramophone records and their wide dispersion by television and radio; the tape recorder (which improves on the gramophone record because it enables the student to respond); automated teaching by programmed instruction; and, penetrating all these techniques, the digital computer.

How will these techniques change patterns of education? This is my first theme; and it concerns the means of education. My second theme is the influence of technology upon the ends of education. This is not a new problem, but it has recently acquired an entirely new significance.

In terms of the influence of technology on the methods of education, it is technological advance—the transistor, the videotape, the computer—which makes the fourth educational revolution possible. It is social advance—egalitarianism and the revolt against elites —which makes the revolution necessary. Less than two generations ago the opportunities for education were sufficient for the demand. There was little talk in those days about shortage of teachers or lack of accommodation. Therefore there was no need to examine critically the technology of education. All this has changed. In many countries today there is a grave shortage of teachers, especially in universities and colleges of technology, and the demand for postsecondary education outruns finance, accommodation, and equipment. In some places it assumes the dimensions of an intellectual famine. It is not surprising that nations are beginning to pay attention to the technology of education and to ask where the application of scientific analysis to educational systems is likely to be rewarding, and where it could be irrelevant or damaging.

The first impact of the educational explosion is the realisation that teachers and buildings must be used as efficiently as possible. Efficiency is a dangerous word to link with education unless it is used with care. Criteria of efficiency appropriate to a bakery cannot be transferred to a cottage kitchen (if they could it would lead to the conclusion that there ought to be no cottage kitchens but communal kitchens for whole rows of cottages). And criteria appropriate to the culture of oranges do not apply to the culture of children. But we are however living in an educational revolution and, just because there are certain dangers, we would be foolish to reject out of hand the scientific style of thinking which has improved so many other useful arts: medicine, architecture and agriculture. In British agriculture, for example, the output of food per agricultural worker per year increased by 53 per cent between 1951 and 1961. If one makes a similar crude comparison of the output of graduates per university teacher over a similar period one finds that productivity has not risen: it has declined (Woodhall and Blaug, 1965). The comparison is crude, and some academics indignantly object to such comparisons being made at all. But I suggest that the contrast does justify us in asking a modest question: do modern technologies enable us to make better use of our limited supply of teachers?

Any technology which increases the rate of learning enables the teacher to teach less and the learner to learn more. There is no doubt that the devices called "audio-visual aids" do contribute to this end. They provide two channels of access to the mind which can be used simultaneously, through the eye and the ear. Consider the tape recorder. There is no doubt that the student learns a foreign language more easily when the eye, on the book, is reinforced by the ear, listening to tape recordings. And in a language laboratory the student can record his own voice, listen to it himself and hear his teacher's comment on it. Though even tape recorders have their abuses, as an American story indicates: A professor had to be away for the last three of his lectures, so he had them put on tape and asked his students to come at the usual time to attend the lectures. He came back unexpectedly in time to give the last of the three lectures in person. There as arranged, was the tape recorder set for giving his lecture, but there were no students: on the seats there were a hundred tape recorders ready to take his lecture down!

As a teaching aid (with emphasis on the word "aid": it is not a substitute for the teacher) the tape recorder, which can bring not only foreign languages but whole courses of lectures into the student's own room, is an educational tool of great promise. So is closed-circuit television, whereby the gifted teacher can speak and offer demonstrations to a far larger audience than he could reach by traditional techniques. And a further development is the video-disc, about the size of a gramophone record and costing about three dollars, which provides the student with a half-hour television lesson. Americans have been at great pains to discover whether students learn as much from televised lectures and videotapes as they do from "live" lectures. They find that it makes no difference whether the lecturer is "live" or on a screen, provided the lecturer has before him a live audience and is responding to the feedback from his listeners. This is not surprising, for these techniques do not involve any novelty in learning theory.

Programmed instruction, however, does involve novel ideas in learning theory, and its efficacy is not yet proven. Skinner (1938) demonstrated how pigeons could be taught to perform quite astonishing feats—such as pecking out a tune on a toy piano—provided they were trained in very small steps taken one at a time, and provided each successful step was rewarded with a grain of corn. The reward, which he called reinforcement, was essential. This led him to suggest that children, too, could be taught complex subjects by breaking the subjects up into very small steps, presenting the steps in the right order, and reinforcing success at each step, not with corn or ice cream but by telling the child immediately that his performance is correct. (This is not a new teaching technique: it is familiar to amateur botanists as the principle of the artificial key to a flora. When you use an artificial key to identify an unknown plant, you are using a kind of book in which the learner is obliged to participate. The same technique can be applied to learning elementary organic chemistry, or statistics, or psychology, by what is called a "scrambled book," or by a machine which presents the alternatives on film instead of on paper.)

Skinner's suggestion is correct. Children do behave like pigeons. And this is why the technique is so dangerous. Pigeons can be taught to play the piano but they cannot be taught to understand music; and except for very limited purposes (such as the memorizing of telephone numbers) rote learning without understanding is useless. The weakness of programmed instruction is that it not only rewards rote learning but, and worse than that, it rewards only those responses which are in agreement with the programme. There is no need to emphasise the perils of that sort of conformity. The doubter, the dissenter, the questioner—in short, anyone with an original mind—can get no stimulus or satisfaction out of the programme. Furthermore, the declared aim of those who compose programmes is to make the steps so simple that the learner does not make mistakes, and so gets his reinforcement at every step; but making mistakes is an essential experience in learning: if you want to train a rat to run a maze, it is no use stopping up all the holes except the right one. In brief, the analogy with pigeons, though correct so far as it goes, goes in the wrong direction. I am reminded of T. H. Huxley's acid criticism of the examination system as it was in England a century ago. Examinees, he said, work to pass, not to know, and nature takes her revenge: they do pass and they don't know.

But we must be patient about programmed learning, for it is still in the primitive stage comparable to that of type in Gutenberg's first book and coachwork in Daimler's first automobile. If we could devise really sophisticated machines which could conduct a dialogue with the student and not merely reward him when he gives the orthodox response, then there are doubtless certain dreary stretches of didactic teaching which a student could be expected to get from a machine in his own time; and this would release the teacher for more subtle (and far more important) activities of teaching. We know already that machines as sophisticated as this can be devised with more facts at their fingertips than any teacher could have, and even with some capacity for encouraging dissent. At present such a machine would be many orders of magnitude more expensive than a teacher (a first class teacher can be trained from birth to graduation for about $60,000). Moreover, its life expectancy would be only about one-eighth that of a teacher. But before the end of this century such machines will certainly be on the market. Just what part they play in the fourth educational revolution will depend on the skill which goes into the programming. A great deal of research will be necessary before we have a theory of teaching which enables us to prepare programmes properly. I doubt whether the machines will be really useful until we understand how the human brain codes information (you could not programme even a simple computer unless you understood how it coded information); and we are still quite in the dark about the coding process in the human brain.

The development of the computer will make sophisticated teaching machines possible; and it is bound to revolutionise education in other ways as well. But have you considered the dangers of successful computers? For instance, a computer with a plausible programme or a political "opinion" could influence the public through a new sort of mass education. Computer-aided predictions of election results are a form of mass education; but education can do harm as well as good. A computerised election prediction tells the man-in-the-street which way the political tide is running. The advertising trade has conditioned him to swim with the tide; so the group of people who publish the prediction may (unconsciously or even deliberately) influence thousands of votes. And there may be the same danger even in traditional forms of education if they are programmed by these techniques for the use of, perhaps, millions of pupils. The groups of people who may, in the future, control the sophisticated programming of curricula, especially in the humanities and social sciences, may come to have a terrifyingly powerful influence on the minds of the young. The programme put out by great educational syndicates could become the new orthodoxy. In a nation where there is freedom of thought and a great diversity of textbooks there is no serious risk that the whole teaching profession will impose one monolithic system of orthodoxy. But commercialised computer education may require us to protect the young even in a democracy against the dangers of orthodoxy. Already in the United States some companies, with a great deal of capital behind them, have been formed for the purpose of "selling education" on a massive scale. If they succeed, programmes of education may be imposed upon us as ruthlessly as detergents are today.

This raises one fear about the fourth educational revolution which I do not share: the fear that it will put teachers out of work. Five centuries of the printed book have not diminished the need for the lecture, seminar, and tutorial. In most fields of knowledge—even in science and technology—the intuitive value judgement, the leap of imagination, and the processing of data by analogy rather than by deduction, are characteristic of the best kind of education. We know no way to elicit these except through dialogue between the teacher and the pupil. The most precious qualities transmitted from teacher to pupil are not facts and theories, but attitudes of mind and styles of thinking. These qualities demand continuous exposure of the pupil to the teacher over long periods, with the subtle effects which come from weekly correction of essays and comments during seminars: the slow progress toward what I regard as the supreme ends of academic higher education, namely mastery of words as symbols of ideas and of signs as symbols of mathematics, and mastery of the dialectic between orthodoxy and dissent which enables man constantly to reexamine and reassess knowledge.

While we must be on our guard, therefore, against naive applications of scientific analysis to the concept of the efficiency of teachers, the scientific approach is safe and has already yielded modest results in two other areas of university efficiency. One is the optimum use of facilities. The Americans have been taking this problem very seriously. They not only collect and analyse data; they also promote large scale experiments to make fuller use of university and school buildings. The results of their experiments are encouraging. Many institutions, ranging from small liberal arts colleges to universities with enrolments of over fifteen thousand, have rearranged their academic year to increase the use of their buildings and equipment. The main effect of these experiments is to increase the rate of flow of students through higher education. The schemes require more staff (though the cost per graduate is probably no greater), but they do not require the staff to work any harder. Indeed some of the schemes have evident advantages for the staff, for they offer blocks of time free from teaching and administration, when teachers can get on with their research and even spend time in other universities where there are better facilities for research.

A second area for employing scientific principles is in applying the concepts of communication theory to educational planning. We are now reconciling ourselves to the idea that education is not a private responsibility, and that in planning it we must take account of manpower needs and economic conditions. Within the general framework of democratic government, schools and colleges constitute a self-regulating system. The system should change in response to a feedback of information, from governments, employers, parents, and students. It is a system much too complicated to yield to rigid mathematical treatment (although simplified models of the system are being treated mathematically—Stone, 1966), but some of the ideas used in communication theory can nevertheless be fruitful for efficient planning. Thus a self-regulating system must be sensitive to the information it receives, so that the content of courses, the balance of subjects taught, and the the distribution of students among different disciplines, may respond to the circumstances of the nation. But the system must not be too sensitive; unless there is some inertia the system will become unstable. I suppose resistance to change is the besetting sin of educational systems; so it is comforting to recognise that there are virtues in inertia. The condition for success of a self-regulating system is that the information fed back to the system automatically sets the control in the right position to respond to the information. If this is to happen in an education system without constant and exasperating vacillations of policy, the information has to include an estimate of the rate of change to which the system must adapt itself. Thus, to take a very simple example, information that a thousand more engineers are needed cannot elicit a satisfactory response from an educational system. But information that the output of engineers should increase by five percent a year over a five-year period is information to which the system can respond. The regulation of an educational system is complicated by the fact that there is an inevitable lag period between receiving information and producing a response: it takes a university four years or more to produce an engineer and by the time the response comes, there may be fresh feedbacks of information which make the response inappropriate. The matter is complicated still further by the unprecedented changes in national policy, so that feedback is not only constantly changing but it also shows few discernible trends. These difficulties will remain, but in the past the chief difficulty has been that there has been no efficient system of feedback and response. Thus—to give one example —although Britain has had possessions in tropical Africa for over a century, and the need for a widespread understanding of African culture has been evident for generations, it was only in 1961 that a government committee recommended the establishment of several centres of African studies in Britain (*Oriental, East European and African Studies;* see also Ashby, 1966).

This concept of self regulation, where one of the responses which an educational system should make to the feedback it receives is to adapt the content of its courses to the needs of the society it serves, introduces my last theme: the impact of technology on curricula in higher education.

Technology is no newcomer to higher education; medicine, one of the oldest technologies, was taught in the university at Salerno in the thirteenth century. The characteristic of technologies is that they began as useful arts without science (the art of healing, the art of building temples and churches, the art of building roads and bridges, the art of war); it is only late in their history that scientific principles have been so vigorously applied to them. The art of teaching is one of the last of the useful arts to become technological. This characteristic shows the nature of technologies: they are not just the application of science to social needs; they are expressions of humanism. Today, in Britain at any rate, the scientific content of technologies is so heavily emphasized that their human content is neglected. Here is one example. Professors of engineering in Britain assert proudly that by the time their graduates are forty years of age many of them (from some universities 70 percent of them) are no longer doing engineering, they are managers or directors or administrators dealing not with machines but with men and women. But in the curricula of the engineering faculties of most British universities there is only lukewarm recognition of this fact. The university may offer voluntary lectures on humanities and social science for scientists and technologists, but it is still uncommon to find, as an integral and examinable part of an engineering course, material on industrial history, social psychology, labour relations, or political institutions; and it is very rare to find any obligation on students in technology to reflect on the ethics of leadership or to consider in a scholarly way such values as justice, magnamity, virtue, and the whole traffic of relations between man and man. Is it assumed that an understanding of these values has been acquired at school? Or that for the practice of technology, it is unnecessary to understand them? Neither assumption would be correct.

It would be totally unrealistic to pretend that the teaching of technology as applied science could or should be reduced; its splendid achievements in this century are due to the application of science. But this is no justification for crowding out of the curriculum the teaching of technology as humanism. The human element in technology is no frill. As machines become more sophisticated the human problems of technology become more challenging. One needs only to look at British industry to see that its chief technological weakness is not that the machines are primitive but that our understanding of industrial sociology is primitive. High wages, commerical television, bingo, and greyhound racing act as sedatives for human problems created by technology, but they do not solve these problems. These unsolved problems cannot be studied in the design office; the place to study them is in the seminar on social philosophy and in the literature class, reading Shakespeare's tragedies, Gogol's novels, and Ibsen's plays. This train of argument leads me to the conclusion that an undergraduate course in technology which does not include a serious element of humanities and social sciences is simply not meeting the needs of society. This conclusion is valid not only in advanced countries, it is equally valid in developing countries. The critical technology in many African states is agriculture. It is a grave deficiency that much of African agriculture is hopelessly unscientific; but a close examination of the problems of African agriculture reveals that the miserable stagnation of much of African farming is due not to lack of science but to the operation of tribal laws for the inheritance of land and cattle. A realistic technology of African agriculture should therefore include social anthropology, sociology, and customary law: these factors are as important as nitrogen, phosphorus, and potash.

That is one reason why humanism and the social sciences are inseparable from the physical sciences in technological education. There is another reason resting in the nature of technology itself. A scientist works by isolating very few variables from a whole situation and drawing conclusions about cause and effect among these variables. He cannot succeed without abstraction from reality. From the point of view of the administrator, the scientist oversimplifies. Thus in my own field of interest there are some delightful (I use the word deliberately) and elegant mathematical theories of evolution. They are worth reading as an aid to clarification and precision of thought, but they have practically no relevance to the actual process of evolution as read in the fossil record. This privilege of oversimplification is one of the accepted conventions of science and is abundantly justified by its results. But technology enjoys no such privilege. One cannot design a radio set without paying attention to appearance, which involves aesthetics; or to its cost, which involves economics; or to the use which people will make of it, which involves sociology and public policy over broadcasting. Human problems are woven into the very texture of technology.

The grand tradition of western education used to be that every educated man drew his culture from the same well. This was his equipment for living in society. The common well of culture from Italy to Scotland contained waters from Judea, Greece, and Rome. In Europe this is no longer true; education has become so diversified and specialised that it no longer transmits a European culture: it transmits only fragments of a culture. I believe this is the cause of many of our international tensions. Is it possible to reconcile the need for specialisation in science and technology with the need for a common core of culture? I think it is.

The solution is not to seek for eternal truths, because Christians, Jews, Muslims, and those with no religious convictions at all, are not likely to agree on what the eternal truths are; but there are eternal *issues* never more sharply focussed than they are today: urban decay, race hatred, the continued contrast between famine in one area and surplus in another, and the hovering fear of environmental crisis or nuclear war. All these problems are intensified by the achievements of science and technology. How can education contribute to their understanding and solution? Surely by introducing the humanities into a scientific education, in such a way as to emphasise the ethical and social consequences of technological achievement: that you cannot build a road, or an airstrip, or a radio transmitter, without profoundly changing the lives of men and women. It is the injection of ideas such as these into technology and politics which may yet carry the western world into the next century without disaster.

Chapter IV

✿✿✿✿✿✿✿✿✿✿✿✿✿✿✿✿✿✿✿✿✿✿✿✿✿✿✿✿✿✿

Hands Off the
University?

The problems of integrating and coordinating universities into a coherent system of higher education occur in every country. How Britain has used academics as members of its major coordinating board—the University Grants Committee—illustrates one approach to assuring creative interaction between the state and higher education.

This chapter may need some gloss for readers unfamiliar with the financing of British universities, which are by right au-

tonomous corporations under royal charters, but which in fact receive more than three-quarters of their income from Parliament. This contrast between theory and practice is reconciled in a typically British manner. Parliament (on the advice of the Department of Education and Science) determines what total sum shall be alloted to the universities. Authority to distribute this sum is delegated to a small body of people, the University Grants Committee, who, apart from the chairman, are not civil servants but are predominantly academics, with a leavening of industralists and persons with responsibility for education in schools. Thus the predominant loyalty of the committee members is to the beneficiaries of the parliamentary grant, not to the paymasters. This pattern of finance has worked well since it was established in 1919, and it is the envy of academics in other countries. But academics are notoriously querulous and the University Grants Committee is perpetually peppered with criticism, a lot of it captious, some of it plain irresponsible. Of course any group of people distributing public funds to importunate enthusiasts will make mistakes and will—and should—be criticised. But in the late 1960s some of this criticism threatened public confidence in the committee, and it was desirable for someone to come to the committee's defence. My qualifications for doing so were that I had served on the University Grants Committee for eight years, and as vice-chancellor (the equivalent of president in an American university) of two universities (Belfast until 1959, and Cambridge from 1967 to 1969). So I had first-hand experience of being both one of the benefactors and one of the beneficiaries.

In January 1966 *The Listener* published a broadcast entitled *Hands off the Universities!* The title was followed by an exclamation mark, which according to the grammar books is used after statements which express emotion. I take the liberty of borrowing the title, but at the end I put not an exclamation mark but a question mark.

Hands off the universities? Whose hands? "The answer to this," according to the broadcast, "is so disturbing that the whole direction in which universities . . . have been developing these last ten years or so is brought into question." The hands which the broadcaster has in mind are dirty and they leave clear fingerprints;

they belong to the Department of Education and Science and to the University Grants Committee. Other academics, too, have identified the fingerprints. One Oxford don, in an article distinguished by the asperity of its abuse rather than by the accuracy of its judgment, writes of the "dead hand of uniformity that the UGC and the Department of Education and Science are busy imposing upon the British universities at large."

Whose hands? The UGC and the DES are not monsters with hands; they are aggregations of men and women. Some of their critics write with an imprecision which would not be tolerated in scholarly works on history or public administration. Where precisely are decisions made in the corridors of academic power? Who makes the decisions? When the critic speaks of universities developing in a "direction," what forces determine this direction?

Bagehot (1963), discussing the government of Britain, wrote that "the observer who looks at the living reality will wonder at the contrast to the paper description." The same could be said of the government of British universities; their statutes and ordinances give little indication of where decisions are made and who makes them. You recollect, I am sure, from your schooldays a problem in textbooks on dynamics. There is a point O, acted upon by three forces represented by straight lines drawn from O and terminating in arrows. The lengths of these lines represent the magnitude of the forces. In which direction will O move? British universities are at point O. Three prime forces act upon them. One force is labelled "the government," which means sometimes the cabinet, sometimes parliament, sometimes the Secretary of State, sometimes civil servants in the DES. A second force is the UGC, together with the research councils which support specific programmes of research in universities. The third force is generated by the inner logic of the universities themselves.

Until recently the movement of point O has been determined primarily by the individual inner logic of each university; in other words, universities have developed—within the resources available to them—as dons in universities wanted them to develop. Until recently the influence of the UGC on the direction of development has been very circumscribed; and the influence of "government" has been (apart from occasional royal commissions and committees of enquiry) confined to certain sporadic acts which certainly affect the *ability* of point O to move, but not the *direction* in which it moves.

For example, opportunities for parliament and cabinet to influence the universities occur once every five years when the scale of recurrent grant is announced, and sporadically during the quinquennium when grants for capital expenditure are announced or when parliament agrees to repair the erosion due to inflation or to finance an increase in the salaries of university teachers. At these points politicians can and do decide the allocation of public expenditure between universities and other forms of postsecondary education. They can have, and I believe they do have, a deliberate policy to limit the overall size of the university system and to divert the surplus of candidates for higher education into institutions in what is unfortunately called "the public sector." Thus, in October 1967 when the Secretary of State announced the recurrent parliamentary grants for the next quinquennium, he said that these grants were to provide for between 220,000 and 225,000 students, but this was about 10,000 students fewer than the estimates prepared by his own department, and 20,000 fewer than the estimates submitted by the universities themselves. This is a perfectly legitimate political decision (whether you agree with it or not is another matter) which politicans have a duty to make. But their prime influence on the universities is confined to making massive grants of money with very few constraints attached to them. None of these constraints impinges on the essential autonomy of the universities. Parliamentary grants have never been coupled with any directive or even innuendo toward the admission of students, the recruitment of staff, the content of courses, the balance of studies, or the standard of examinations. In giving money to the universities, parliament gives them freedom to use the money as they think best. Without this money the universities would have enjoyed the dubious freedom of a pauper. Of course there has not been enough money. More money would mean more freedom. But a critic would have to be paranoically querulous to interpret limitations of finance as interference from politicians.

Whose hands? Certainly not the hands of politicians. What about civil servants? Are their fingerprints on the universities? Now that the DES is the channel of communication between the univer-

sities and parliament there is certainly an opportunity for interference. The faceless men in the DES could, in a score of subtle
ways, influence the movement of point O and never disclose that the
gloved hands on the universities were theirs. But there is an alarm
system: their influence would have to flow through the UGC. So
unless the UGC acquiesces in this influence the universities are safely
insulated from it. For eight years I have served on the UGC and
it is betraying no official secret to say that since the UGC was transferred from the Treasury to the Department there has been continuous consultation between officers of the UGC and civil servants
in Curzon Street, and out of this consultation there do emerge proposals about overall university policy in relation to the rest of higher
education. These proposals are certainly influenced by the views of
those who have to think of the whole educational system of this
nation. But it is also betraying no official secret to say that the prime
initiative for these proposals lies in the UGC not in the DES. The
civil servants in Curzon Street have behaved with admirable pro-
priety; there is not any evidence to support the assertion that the
DES is imposing its "dead hand" (as one critic calls it) on the
universities. The hands, whether alive or dead, are not the hands of
civil servants.

The next potential culprit is already only too obvious. The
hands must be the hands of the UGC. Let us examine these hands.
First, who makes the decisions? Second, what sort of decisions do
they make? The UGC meets in a small, ill-ventilated room in Park
Crescent. Take stock of its members as they drink a cup of anaemic
coffee at eleven o'clock on a Thursday morning: a professor of
German, two professors of history, a professor of economics, a professor of philosophy, a professor of chemistry, two professors of
engineering, a professor of medicine, a professor of zoology, a professor of physics, the heads of an Oxford and of a Cambridge college,
a director of education, a headmistress, and three industrialists,
under the chairmanship of an ex-vice-chancellor: a body comprising
77 percent of academics. These are the people who make decisions
on the UGC. That's all very well, some sceptics say; but the committee members cannot know what is going on. The real decisions
are made by a team of bureaucrats in the office. The committee
members are just a facade. Again, it is betraying no official secret for

me to assert bluntly that these sceptics are talking nonsense. The normal agenda for a UGC meeting weighs about two pounds. It includes material for such major matters as the advice to be given to the government on recurrent grants for the next quinquennium, and on such minor matters as authority for a grant of £200 to a university for furnishing a common room. The committee members undertake to give a fifth of their time to the committee's work; and some give a good deal more. They do their homework. There are a dozen or more subject subcommittees under the chairmanship of committee members but composed of experts in humanities, physical science, biological science, medicine, technology; and other academic experts are constantly being coopted. A bid for equipment from a new department, for instance, is assessed by two experts in the subject, who usually visit the department. The experts are frequently more distinguished in the subject than is the professor whose bid they assess. In a word, decisions made by the UGC are decisions made by academics or on the recommendation of panels of other academics. So here, at last, is the answer to my question. Whose hands? *The hands of other dons.*

Other dons they may be, but are they, perhaps, corrupted by their office? Are they academic quislings? Let me tell you a story which answers this question. The UGC has two quite separate functions: one advisory, one executive. Its advice flows upwards. It recommends to the government how much money the universities need in order to discharge properly their function in the nation; and in recent years its advice has broadened to include recommendations to the government about the discharge of that function. What subjects (such as Latin American studies) should be encouraged? Which universities (such as Nottingham) should be financed to found medical schools? Which towns (such as Lancaster) should become the homes of new universities? Its executive activity flows downwards. It distributes parliamentary grants—with no reference to government—among universities as it thinks fit. And what it thinks fit is that they should be block grants, not—except in unusual cases—earmarked for any specific expenditure. With minor reservations each university is left completely free to allocate its recurrent block grant among the various categories of expenditure according to its own assessment of priorities.

All this is so familiar that it seems otiose to repeat it. Yet *is* it so familiar? Not many months ago the UGC was visiting one of our more famous universities. The Committee was having its usual informal discussion with a group of arts professors. Some of these professors asked, vehemently, that the UGC should earmark part of its grant to their famous university to provide secretarial help for arts professors. The chairman of the UGC swallowed his surprise and said: "But this would mean that your university would surrender to the UGC its freedom to decide how to spend part of its income. Surely you don't mean that." And one of the professors replied, "Yes. We do."

Hands off the universities, indeed! These professors offer the UGC a precious ingredient of autonomy, namely the right of the university to allocate its recurrent grant as it thinks fit! They had to be told pretty sharply that the UGC is here to perserve the autonomy of the universities, not to erode it. This is not an isolated instance: I could tell of others. But perhaps this is enough to demonstrate that dons who join the UGC do not suffer corruption.

Indeed, in its determination to preserve the autonomy of universities, the UGC did not, in the past (it is very different now), give the universities as clear a lead as it could have done (and, as I personally believe, it ought to have done). A number of years ago the Committee of Vice-Chancellors and Principals issued a public statement saying that universities in the future "will be glad to have a greater measure of guidance from the Government than until quite recent days they have been accustomed to receive." Here is an invitation to *dirigisme* from the universities themselves. The UGC has responded by giving guidance, through expert committees, on the need for higher education in subjects such as Oriental and African studies, Russian studies, and Latin American studies. This guidance has been accepted; but over some issues, such as the size of universities, it might have been better if the UGC had overridden university opinion. Some years ago at a Home Universities Conference not one delegate challenged the following statement: "There is no such thing as a right size for a university, but the tendency is likely to be for them to flatten out at roughly the following figures: 4500 (four faculty); 3000 (three faculty); 1750 (two faculty). Universities can only soundly grow larger than this on a collegiate or federal basis."

Also about that time the Association of University Teachers suggested a limit of 4500 students per university, except where that number was already exceeded. The data for disputing these opinions were already available. If the UGC had foreseen then that the critical mass of a university in the 1970s was going to be 10,000–15,000 students, it might have given "guidance" to the great city universities to grow to 10,000 or more; and it might have curbed the proliferation of quite so many new universities, which now present a great financial embarrassment. The fact is that the UGC has had such respect for the autonomy of individual universities and for the wisdom of individual vice-chancellors that it has not, until recently, felt free to regard the universities of Britain as units in a system of higher education to be integrated, coordinated, and considered as a whole. On the contrary, the UGC regarded each university as a good banker regards each of his clients: it has encouraged each university to develop according to its own inner logic. This attitude has inevitably (and rightly, in my view) changed. In 1967, when universities received news of their allocations of grant for the next quinquennium, they also received a "Memorandum of General Guidance." This is a document of historical importance. It emphasises that the UGC does not expect, or seek to achieve, uniformity among universities. It reminds each university that it "is free to determine the distribution of its annual block grant in the light of the guidance . . . which the Committee has given." But the memorandum does set out unambiguously what is expected from British universities in return for the public support they receive. It draws attention to urgent national needs. It enjoins interuniversity collaboration. It warns against needless proliferation of departments in "rare" or expensive subjects. It comments on the need for further thought about postgraduate studies.

None of this guidance could seriously be regarded as eroding the essential components of autonomy in the universities. One such component is university control over the allocation of its recurrent grant. There are three other essential components: control of admission and examination of students, control of curricula, and control of appointment and tenure of academic staff. The British universities have undisputed sovereignty over all three of these components; and nothing the UGC has written or done questions this sovereignty.

What, then, lies behind the alarm that hostile hands are clutching at the universities? I said earlier that the UGC has two functions: executive, which flows downwards to universities, and advisory, which flows upwards to governments. But the UGC has a third function. Because of the confidence reposed in it—a confidence so great that since its foundation until 1968 its accounts were not even subject to parliamentary scrutiny—the UGC has had the responsibility of a trustee for public funds. Its officers have repeatedly had to defend this anomalous position against pressure from politicians and civil servants, who murmur about getting "value for money" from the universities and ask about "efficiency in utilisation of plant." In order to protect the universities from these invisible but continuous pressures the UGC has had to demonstrate that it does exert some control over expenditure. In doing so, its silent plea to the universities has been one laid down years ago by Hilaire Belloc, in one of his Cautionary Tales: "Always keep a hold on nurse, For fear of finding something worse." In doing so, the UGC exposes itself to criticism from persons who talk about the "dead hand of uniformity." Of course examples of uniformity can be quoted. One is the imposition of a structure of salary scales standard for all universities, and an upper limit to the proportion of senior posts which any university may have. The grades of lecturer and assistant lecturer have a salary ladder as rigid as that in the civil service; and the proportion of professors, readers, and senior lecturers must not exceed 35 percent of the whole academic staff. The purpose of these constraints is simple. The salary bill for academic and administrative staff constitutes well over half the recurrent exchequer grant. One simple assurance which the UGC can give to parliament is that there can be no undue extravagance in this large element of expenditure. One only has to look across the Atlantic to see the effects of an unrestrained salary market for dons: universities bidding against one another for some Nobel prizewinner like dealers over an old master at a sale of pictures. Clearly it would be intolerable for universities to compete for staff in this way, using the taxpayer's money. The constraint imposed by the UGC is therefore, one of the UGC's defences for university autonomy. It has another very useful effect: it ensures that a modest, and as yet not very distinguished, university can afford the same ratio of staff to students as a university higher in the peck order of prestige. I myself have some regrets about the degree of rigidity; for the staff-student ratio in British universities is richer, I believe, than similar ratios in any other country. I am not convinced such a high ratio is necessary. It would be an interesting experiment if some British universities could offer better salaries within the total limits of salary expenditure calculated on present practice, by diluting its staff/student ratio. It might be discovered that dons would be willing to accept a heavier teaching load if they got more pay, without prejudicing the quality of their teaching or of their research. This would be a useful discovery, but it is by the way. Some control of expenditure on salaries financed from public funds is essential; if the UGC did not exert it, parliament would. It is one of the defences of university autonomy.

A second example of uniformity concerns the norms for capital expenditure on buildings and equipment. The annual exchequer grant for nonrecurrent expenditure exceeds £100 millions; but this sum is painfully inadequate. Great institutions such as some colleges of the University of London are having to work in obsolescent buildings under conditions of overcrowding and squalor. Would it be fair to allow the University of Barchester to build a residence hall with a bathroom for each student, or a geology department with a private suite for the professor, while some departments of Birkbeck College have to survive in a converted warehouse? The answer to this superfluous question is obvious. But a consequence of the answer is that the UGC must prescribe norms for the size of rooms, for the space needed per student in a laboratory, and for the number of bathrooms in residence halls.

Underlying these constraints there is a simple and important principle, and I concede that it is a principle of uniformity. It is this: The universities of Britain inevitably differ in prestige. It would be disingenuous to deny that some universities are more distinguished (on the curious criteria that dons use for distinction, such as the number of Fellows of the Royal Society per acre) than others. But it is the underlying philosophy of the UGC that *the material opportunities for achieving distinction* should not differ from one university to another. Hence the same salary scales for lecturers in Manchester and in Bath. Hence the similar staff/structure and staff/ student ratio in Bristol and in Hull. Hence the insistence that student accommodation financed by the UGC shall be no more luxurious in Oxford than in Keele. What the UGC does is to guarantee to all universities a minimum—and on international standards it is a very high minimum—level of material support for their educational activities. But this does not mean that the UGC imposes a policy of financial uniformity on universities. The UGC knows and accepts the fact that it costs thirty percent more per student per annum to produce a physics graduate in one university than in another; and the diversity of expenditure is increased still further by grants from research councils, which deliberately support excellence and make no pretence to spread their grants evenly among the universities. But the UGC guarantees a minimum standard. The uniformity so distasteful to some professors is the same kind of uniformity which guarantees that all new public housing has indoor sanitation.

This is not the only charge against the UGC. There is another quite different charge. In recent years the Committee has pestered universities with questionnaires. Not only (it is alleged) do these waste the time of the professors and of administration who have to fill them in; worse than that, they ask questions which could lead to odious comparisons between one university and another: questions about failure rates, the division of effort between research and teaching, and the use made of accommodation. For example, since British universities are carrying a quarter of the responsibility for civil research outside private industry, we clearly should have ways of estimating just what universities do spend on research. Accordingly in 1965 the UGC circulated a request to the universities, asking for a slightly less capricious estimate of the division of effort between teaching and research than the guess that it was about half and half. The request was received with indignation. Some vice-chancellors (men who are supposed to have learnt to weigh their words) described it as "ill-conceived" and a "vexatious waste of time." Commentators asserted that it was this sort of inquisitorial nonsense which undermined confidence in the UGC. Of course it was a tiresome enquiry. It is practically impossible to determine how much effort one puts into research (and anyway in research there is no linear relationship between effort and result). Nevertheless, it is not beyond the wit of a don to substract from the total number of hours he works at his job those hours which go toward teaching or preparation for teaching or on administration, and to say whether he can honestly attribute the remainder to research. This would be a crude estimate of course. The UGC questionnaire was indeed imperfect; it was severely criticised by UGC members. But the inevitable consequence of the protest was that the Committee of Vice-Chancellors set up a subcommittee of its own to work out a better method. The subcommittee also produced a tiresome questionnaire. It worked for months on the response and it did not succeed in producing a better method. The effect on dons will be the same: they will be pestered with more questionnaires, this time from members indubitably of their own tribe. Indeed another questionnaire from the Committee of Vice-Chancellors was circulated asking universities, among other things, for the number of private staff rooms into which two or more undergraduates could be fitted (it didn't specify standing or sitting) and for a comparison between the number of students registered for a class and the number who actually attend (a statistic with rich possibilities for interpretation). In a word, the Committee of Vice-Chancellors, in order to protect universities from the donnish hands of the UGC, found itself obliged to lay its own collective hands on the universities. It is not for me—a vice-chancellor—to say whether this is an improvement or not.

But hands of some sort will inevitably be laid upon the universities. Thus there has recently been a marked increase in what can be called *crypto-dirigisme* over universities. Here are three symptoms of it: First, the government is clearly committed to the view that the universities should be part of a *system* of higher education, and this implies some surrender of sovereignty from individual universities to the system to which they belong. Second, the UGC is responding, in a sense of great responsibility, but with increasing firmness, to the appeal for guidance which the vice-chancellors made a number of years ago. For instance, it has advised three universities to phase out their teaching in agriculture on the ground that there are too many schools of agriculture in Britain, and it is applying strong pressures toward rationalisation of resources in expensive departments such as chemical engineering, "rare" subjects such as African studies, and computers, observatories, and other equipment and facilities. Third, the Comptroller and Auditor General now has access to the accounts of the UGC and the universities.

His officers make visitations to every university and they have the right of access to any persons or records they need for their enquiries. His approach, of course, is very courteous and reassuring. The Comptroller and Auditor General is not an agent of the government. He does not question policy; he examines only the efficiency or otherwise of the way public money is spent on policy as laid down by the authorities in the institution he is investigating. Thus, unless it were UGC policy to insist on uniformity (which it is not) the Comptroller and Auditor General assures us he would not question diversity of expenditure among universities for what appears to be the same purpose: the production, for instance, of a physics graduate. In universities, where decision-making is dispersed among individual departments, he is going to have great difficulty in deciding what the policy *is* which his officers must not question! But I am sure, if dons remain calm and alert, they will be able to create conventions which the Comptroller and Auditor General will respect.

"If dons remain calm." These are all symptoms of *dirigisme,* and there will be more. Dons have a choice of two attitudes toward these symptoms. One is the futile cry: "Hands off the Universities!" The other, and in my view the right one, is to determine that the movement of point O shall still be determined largely by the inner logic of the universities (but acting collectively), yet in such a way that it responds readily to legitimate forces exercised by government and by the UGC and research councils.

This second attitude concedes that hands must be laid on the universities. But it would insist that they should be, as they are already, predominantly the hands of other dons. Why other dons? Why not politicians and civil servants? Have I forgotten that reform in universities has almost invariably had to wait upon the pressures of royal commissions? No, I have not. The interesting fact about royal commissions on universities is that it has been the academic members who have exerted the greatest influence. (Haldane was perhaps an exception, but he was a don in spite of himself.) But there is a valid reason why the hands should be the hands of dons. University teaching is as highly technical as in the practice of medicine. It is right that the layman should say what society expects from its professors and its medical practitioners. It would be crazy for the

layman to tell the professor how to teach or the doctor how to prescribe. So government influence on the movement of point O must
be confined to overall social policy (such as the proportion of the
age group to receive postsecondary education). Apart from this, the
hands must remain the hands of other dons. To safeguard this I am
sure that dons themselves will be willing to adapt their traditional
ideas of what constitutes university autonomy.

Fortunately there are signs that dons are adapting their
traditions. Each of the forty-four universities of Britain is an independent corporation, established by royal charter. But the universities are now beginning to recognise that there is no security in the
fragmented autonomy of four dozen independent corporations. What
is needed is a collective autonomy of *interdependent* corporations,
each of which retains freedom for diversity but which together present a common front on matters of vital importance. This is the only
way in which the universities of Britain can continue to depend on
government funds and yet be strong enough to secure, by collective
bargaining, the conditions necessary to fulfill their function in
society. There are signs that things are moving in this direction. The
Committee of Vice-Chancellors (which in its early days was neurotically afraid of committing its member universities) has of its own
accord dispelled the chaos which formally surrounded the procedure
for admissions to universities; it has done something but not enough
to simplify the levels of achievement required for entry to universities;
it has stimulated a series of investigations into Organisation and
Methods by groups of universities. It has, provoked by the UGC,
embarked on a study of costs of university departments and of utilisation of buildings. It will have to do more. There will have to be an
increase of influence from the centre and a decrease of autarky at
the periphery.

Indeed the best safeguard for the future would be a con-
solidation of hands on the universities: more hands rather than
fewer, provided they are predominantly the hands of dons. I recollect
a time when meetings between representatives of the Committee of
Vice-Chancellors and the UGC comprised a score of men sitting
round the table with a common aim and common convictions. I
recollect, more recently, meetings at which the Vice-Chancellors and
the UGC members seemed to be ranged on two "sides," man-

oeuvring round one another like boxers in a ring. This recent attitude is deplorable. In partnership the UGC and the Committee of Vice-Chancellors are a powerful combination; divided they invite attack from the enemies of learning. And let us never forget that there are enemies of learning in Britain.

Finally, let us not forget that the health of a university depends on whose hands are on it *inside* its own walls. One of the unsolved problems of university government is how to involve younger academics in the academic society. Hierarchies, with deans and professors making most of the decisions, are so tidy and simple and convenient that there are professors who want their own junior staff to keep their hands off the universities too. Iconoclastic lecturers with revolutionary ideas, one is told, can waste much time. But in that attitude danger lies. All the arguments which convince us as a nation that democracy is preferable to fascism are equally valid in a university. A university is a society which cannot run except as an inverted hierarchy. The ideas well up from below. The money flows down from above.

Hands off the universities? No. That would be nonsense in the 1970s. But let them remain the hands of other dons.

Chapter V

❀❀❀❀❀❀❀❀❀❀❀❀❀❀❀❀❀❀❀❀❀❀❀❀❀❀❀❀❀❀❀❀❀

Influence of
Students

The essence of a university education at its highest is to train students to advance knowledge by disputing accepted theories and challenging traditions. If we ask them to apply this training to disciplines like chemistry or history, we must not be surprised if they apply it also to the university itself. This attitude of disputation, challenge, and intellectual rebellion, provided it is genuine and sincere and constructive, can be beneficial to the university. But it is essential to distinguish the rebel who has integrity from the rebel who is frivolous or only out to make mischief.

60

When the common seal of the University of Cambridge is affixed to any contract or agreement, the document is signed on behalf of the *chancellor, masters, and scholars*. This trinity constitutes the corporation. If there were an Athanasian Creed for universities, it would declare that in this trinity, too, "none is greater or less than another." All are coequal. And the academic equivalent of the Arian heresy is to deny this coequality, although in divers times and places universities have fallen into this heresy.

The universities of Italy began seven centuries ago as societies of students. Representatives of the students negotiated with the civic authorities. They hired and paid the professors. They even exacted fines from the professor if he lectured too long or came late to his class; and to prevent his accepting an attractive offer from a neighbouring university, he sometimes had to deposit cash with the students' representative.

Vestiges of the pattern of Italian student universities survive to this day. In Scottish universities the students elect the rector; and the rector, though he is primarily an honorific figure who delivers an address under somewhat trying conditions, has nevertheless important statutory rights. He can and does appoint an assessor, who sits on the university governing body, and he may and sometimes does take the chair at governing body meetings. In other universities influenced by the Scottish tradition—the University of Sydney, for instance, and the Queen's University of Belfast—the president of the students' representative council, if a graduate, has a seat on the university governing body.

The two ancient English universities follow a different medieval pattern, which originated in Paris. The scholars are formally members of the trinity, but effective government is in the hands of the masters. Students do not, and never did, play a part in university government. As for the civic universities of Britain, they all have student organisations which influence, though they do not control university affairs.

The academic Arian heresy—the concept of the university as a research institute—came from Germany in the nineteenth century. Universities have always contained men of great intellectual curiosity who have worked at the advancing frontiers of knowledge; and a spirit of research, as contrasted with the mere publication of papers, is inseparable from good teaching. But the German professor converted this natural and commendable activity into a fetish, and for a time some British academics imitated him. With his research students, he was on informal, easy terms. But too often he resented the time spent on elementary teaching. In 1908 Friedrich Paulsen, the historian of the German universities, wrote: "The principle that the scholars and investigators of the nation shall also be the teachers of the youth has triumphed." But a few lines further on he is quoting the professor who regards the term as a tiresome interruption of the vacation. And, nearer home, who has not heard the university teacher in Britain who says: "My teaching load is so heavy this year that I'll not be able to get down to my own work!" As though the task of teaching undergraduates is not worth dignifying by the title "my own work."

For various reasons, all of which are familiar, some departments in some British universities did go through a phase of academic Arianism, when they did not regard the scholars as coequal with the masters. I think we have emerged from that phase now. Books and articles about universities are now almost neurotically preoccupied with some aspects of student life. The Robbins Committee in 1963 published 963 pages about them in an appendix to its report. The University Grants Committee set up a subcommittee to study how they are taught. Other writers have analysed how they perform at examinations, how they use their time, how they make their friends, how they spend their money. And we all go through agonies of self-examination as to how we should select them. In America sociologists study student cultures with that humourless intensity previously reserved for research into the habits of primitive Polynesian tribes. Examples abound of American studies of campus sociology, all quantified, with means and standard deviations and chi-square tests on ego achievement, narcissism, sex prudery, deference, and succorance-autonomy (whatever that is). All this enquiry is laudable and perhaps necessary. At least it demonstrates that we take students seriously; but it concerns mainly the influence of universities upon students. My theme here is the influence of students upon universities.

We must distinguish two kinds of influence. The management of universities is now so complex and time consuming that it is impractical to expect students to take a major part in the executive acts of university government. Indeed some educators think that the administration of universities is too complex to be entrusted even to the masters. But students can influence university government without becoming involved in its mechanism. The case I am now going to make is that students are already exerting a beneficial influence on universities; that they should be encouraged to exert more; and that through this influence their coequality in the academic trinity should be manifest.

The distinguished American sociologists Burton Clark and Martin Trow (1966) describe four subcultures among American students. With some anglicising modifications they are found in Britain too. There is, first, the student who comes to college primarily to take part in social and athletic activities and with no interest in intellectual life: a species common enough in Oxford and Cambridge fifty years ago, but now happily so rare as to have become a collector's piece. Second, there is the student who comes to college solely to get a ticket for a job. He is no more interested in the university which sells him knowledge than he is in the supermarket which sells him coffee. The words "and scholars" mean nothing to him. He does not belong to a society; he is shopping for a diploma. He, unhappily, is not so rare. But let us not blame him, as we are so often tempted to do. It is our fault; our social climate makes him as he is. My generation has encouraged higher education to become an instrument for social mobility, and we can hardly blame our children for using it that way.

Neither of those subcultures has much influence on the university in Britain, the one because it is almost extinct, the other because it repudiates its full membership in the society. But there are two other subcultures: one is the dedicated academic, who comes to the university to find the values for which universities exist, who is loyal to its traditional purposes and impatient of its imperfections. He takes seriously his partnership in the trinity of chancellor, masters, and scholars. He is willing to become involved in university problems and prestige. (This student, too, may enthusiastically play rugby or cricket, he may row in the first eight, but these activities are ancillary to his work; also he may be ambitious to get a good degree, but he takes this in stride in his eager pursuit of knowledge.)

Finally there is the rebel, deeply involved in ideas and in politics, with a lively and angry social conscience and with many of his interests outside the university, often ostentatiously trying to withdraw himself from college affairs but always drawn back by his aggressive nonconformism which brings him up against authority, because he feels it is his duty to display a generalised hostility to the establishment. He despises tradition; and his final gesture is to take his degree in absentia because he can't stand the mumbo-jumbo of the graduation ceremony. Whereas the dedicated academic is a willing partner, although maybe a critical one, in fulfilling the narrow and traditional social purpose of the university, the rebel is forever blurring the distinction between the university and the world and wants to involve the university in uncomfortably controversial affairs. Both these subcultures, the academic and the rebel, have significance for the trinity. For them the words "and scholars" are living words.

In all British universities except Oxford and Cambridge there are formal channels of communication between the scholars on the one hand and the chancellor (or at any rate the vice-chancellor) and masters on the other. Students through their elected councils (the students' representative council or the guild or the union) are in constant touch with the establishment. They pass resolutions. They compose memoranda. They press for participation. Each student council prepares a statement which is submitted to the University Grants Committee for its quinquennial visitation. In connection with these visitations I have studied the statements from student student councils in most of the British universities. I would now like to give my assessment of the quality of their thought, the range of their interests, and the extent of their influence.

There are two striking features about the statements: their maturity and their frankness. Although they contain requests that the University Grants Committee should finance theatres, new unions, swimming baths, boat houses, lavatories in the sports pavilion, and psychiatrists on the campus, these are clearly regarded as subsidiary matters, stuck into the end of the statement. Almost without exception the statements give pride of place to academic affairs: the quality of teaching, tutorial work, staff-student contacts, the library. One begins by saying that at this time of expansion the university must not lose sight of its original aim, to provide a liberal education; "we feel deeply that we should remain a homogenous and balanced university." Another asserts that a university must be "a community in which all members may pursue their chosen studies . . . in an atmosphere of learning." Another deplores the retreat from the broad-based Scottish M.A. degree in favour of narrow-based special degrees. On teaching, students have some timely suggestions: for instance, that committees dealing with appointments and promotions should take into account the candidate's skill as a teacher and his interest in students, and that lecturers should be given leaves of absence to have instruction in teaching methods. They unanimously appeal for more tutorial classes and discussions, and among particular suggestions are weekend residential conferences between staff and students, a "reading term" in the summer, and an undertaking that lectures should not be given on subjects adequately covered in textbooks.

The chief dissatisfaction is over what is ambiguously described as staff-student relations. I suppose the prime pedagogical problem in a university is how to bridge the gap between two generations. The evidence from students shows how commonly we fail. From one student council comes a dry comment about the futility of "artificially contrived situations" such as sherry parties. Informal and unpremeditated opportunities for conversation are needed so that exchanges which begin in the classroom can be continued outside, in joint common rooms, cafés and pubs. Staff willing to entertain in their homes should be given an entertainment allowance. But many professors and lecturers (says another statement), though admirably qualified to teach in their special fields, are poorly qualified to contribute to the wide aims of the university community. All of us who have taught in universities wonder sometimes whether students ever want to see us outside the classroom or the laboratory. And, if the truth be told, we wonder, too, why they want to see us. It appears, surprising as it may seem, that they do, provided the encounter is not contrived and is not regarded by either masters or scholars as duty. This, I believe, is a great compliment to the academic profession, and a challenge too.

These statements to the University Grants Committee cover many other topics which are surprising unless one regards students as adults. One student council wants students to have one or two years in a job before coming to the university; another wants much better information distributed to schools about university subjects which are not taught in schools; another wants weekend courses on careers for sixth-form boys once they have been given university places. There is an appeal for larger and better libraries and more free time for using them. Not only the teaching, but the buildings, come in for comment. "We deplore," says one statement, "the way appearance has taken precedence over convenience" in the halls of residence. And there is a strong current of opinion in favour of bed-sitters, student flats, and student villages rather than conventional halls of residence.

Let us look now at another source of student opinion. The National Union of Students was founded in 1922 and has 480 institutions affiliated with it, representing over two hundred thousand students. From time to time it comes in for criticism as a body which attracts the student-politician and uses up a lot of time which its delegates might profitably spend at their studies. But examine its recent record. It arranges a drama festival; it helps and finances some voluntary service in developing countries; it organises charter flights abroad for over ten thousand students; it prepares reports on such topics as local authority awards, housing, and vacation work; it submitted a report to the University Grants Committee on university expansion, and memoranda to the Anderson Committee on students' grants, the Hale Committee on teaching, the Jones Committee on audio-visual aids, and the Robbins Committee. Its recommendations to the Robbins Committee are sober, eloquent, and (although in the climate of opinion at the time this is perhaps not remarkable) they bear a reasonable resemblance to the recommendations eventually made by the Robbins Committee itself. Its submission to the Hale Committee contains no arguments for easier courses or predigested information. Let the lecturer talk (they say) about what interests him, and let the student get the routine stuff out of books. And on tutorials the National Union of Students says something which might well apply (though only the boldest man would mention it) in the quadrangles and courts of Oxford and Cambridge: "We are concerned that often that which passes as a tutorial system or personal supervision amounts to no more than a series of individual problem-solving sessions." The submission also urges that tutorials must "arouse the intellectual curiosity of the student, to develop a healthy spirit of criticism." The National Union of Students is in one sense ahead of the British government, for it unites in one community students of all sorts—from colleges of education, technical colleges, colleges of art, and universities. Much of the malaise in British higher education is due to the fact that at every level except that of the students, these diverse institutions of higher education have not been combined into a system.

The scope and quality of student opinion in Britain today indicates that although these young men and women do not have the expertise to run universities (the art of academic government needs a long and austere apprenticeship), they do know how they want universities to be run; and after a lifetime in universities I believe their ideas are by and large sound and viable. I believe too that the expressions of student opinion which I have summarised have a significant and healthy influence on British higher education. To speak from my own experience, the discussions which the University Grants Committee has with groups of undergraduates on its visitations to universities are illuminating and helpful and in recent years have certainly influenced decisions on policy. Also, in some universities in recent years, the scholars have been taken into the confidence of the masters and have been consulted on aspects of university policy before decisions are made.

These changes reassure us that the academic Arian heresy is a thing of the past. But we have to acknowledge that this highly responsible, highly adult student opinion comes from a minority of the scholars. Although Trow's classification of students is (like all taxonomic systems) a gross oversimplification, it illustrates how difficult it is going to be to regard a university as a corporation which includes all the scholars, not just a minority of them.

Many university students are not prepared to identify themselves with the corporation to which they belong. They are not excluded from partnership in the trinity; they abdicate from it and withhold their loyalty. The students likely to identify themselves with university or college are, first, those who still regard it solely as a finishing school where they can polish their social manners, join dining clubs, and row before going into father's business; and, second, those who have a genuine interest in academic affairs and enthusiasm for learning. Students in the first category are, as I have said, nearly extinct and in any case are disenchanted with the modern university, which (to the disgust of some of the alumni) now expects that students get degrees. The second category is the source of much of the sound judgment and balanced criticism which I have drawn upon as data to illustrate my theme. It includes the student who earnestly wants the university to maximise the opportunities for a liberal education. But there remain the two subcultures which reject the partnership: the "ticket men" and the rebels. These challenge the assumptions on which universities stand. Universities cannot afford to disregard this challenge. Let us face it for a moment here.

Our success in removing the financial barriers to higher education has created another social problem. Thousands of students in Britain today are exposing themselves to higher education because to accept the university place as the line of least resistance. They are not at universities because they are interested in learning, or even because their parents were ambitious on their behalf. They were examinees at school and they have been drafted by the offer of local authority awards. Their purpose—if you can drag it out of them—is to get a degree and to get out. America has a similar problem, as Clark and Trow (1966) recognise: "The central problems of mass higher education are not the problems of measuring and identifying talent, financing expansion, or raising faculty salaries. . . . Rather the central problems are student boredom, their indifference and hostility to learning, and the irrelevance of their associations and relationships with other students to their education. . . . Hundreds of thousands of students from culturally impoverished backgrounds and with narrow vocational interests enter college for the many jobs and occupations which now call for college diplomas, but without any marked enthusiasm, curiosity, originality, or involvement with ideas and learning."

Student councils in British universities would unanimously endorse this diagnosis. Their commonest indictment of their fellow students is apathy. The only virtue of the apathetic student—if you can call it a virtue—is that he doesn't cause trouble. Teachers don't care for him. Employers don't want him. He debases the idea of a university, and to this extent he is (I believe) a menace to our expanding system of higher education, for if he spreads he will cause public disillusionment with universities. Already the University Grants Committee has taken steps to arouse the apathetic student: it encourages students to reside in communities; it resists the nine-to-five attitude to university life; it supports extracurricular activities; it advocates less specialisation in curricula. I wish more could be done. The best hope is in an extension of studies on the motivation of students. If we could infect students with motivation or ruthlessly eliminate students with inadequate motivation, I believe we would be making a major contribution to the health of our universities. For a start could we not place greater emphasis than we do on the fact that a university is a society of chancellor, masters, and scholars, coequal in importance, and that there are equally compelling obligations on all three constituents of the society? To accept these obligations should be a condition of membership.

And, lastly, the rebels. Let me declare myself at once and say that, with one reservation, I am in favour of rebels. After all, a university education at its highest is one which teaches a person how to advance knowledge by disputing accepted theories and challenging traditions. You can't teach young people to question established fact and not expect them to question the establishment.

But a genuine rebel is an individualist whose actions arise from his own inner conscience. There is also in universities a phoney rebel, the student who joins a nonconformist cult, who is simply showing off, who shows (though it may not be his fault) the symptoms of a contagious emotional disturbance. He is not easily distinguished from the genuine rebel. Perhaps one diagnostic sign is his determination to reject all social norms indiscriminately, whether they concern important issues, such as pacifism versus patriotism, or trivial issues, such as the compulsory wearing of gowns. An undergraduate who is prepared to suffer for his views on nuclear disarmament or racial equality is (in my view) fulfilling the prime purpose of an intellectual community, which is continually to examine and to challenge major assumptions made by society. An undergraduate who is prepared to suffer for his views on wearing a collar and tie at dinner or on the hours at which girls may visit his room is (in my view) simply lacking in perspective and judgment; if you insist on going back to first principles on the trivia of life, you have no time or energy to question first principles on the fundamentals.

But, subject to this reservation, let us welcome the genuine rebel scholar. It is not easy to welcome him. Any sympathetic approach from vice-chancellors or masters he regards with a suspicious and a jaundiced eye (he cannot conceive that many of them were rebels, too, in their day). He is impatient of what may appear to be compromise or appeasement. The tortuous diplomacy which leads to academic decision-making he regards as sheer weakness. He is not prepared to play a subtle game of chess with the establishment; he would rather pick up the chessboard and bang the establishment over the head with it. Never mind. If he is a genuine rebel he is worth his weight in gold. He must be taught the techniques of successful dissent. Above all he must be persuaded not to abdicate from the society of masters and scholars. His ideas—raw and repetitive as they may seem to old men—must be nurtured and gently disciplined by drawing them into the channels of administrative action.

Beside the difficulty of approaching the rebel scholar, he presents other problems to the masters. He is separated from them by events which are barriers to communication, more formidable than we realise. I remember, as a middle-aged man, in Moscow, hearing the news from the famous physicist Peter Kapitza that the bomb had been dropped on Hiroshima; and I remember our both coming to the conclusion that we were already at that time too old to adjust ourselves completely to that event. A few years ago I had a party of undergraduates in my house. Before they came I looked at their files and saw that most of them were born in the year Hiroshima was bombed. They have never known a world which was not trembling at just below flash point. This fact still dominates the thoughts of those of them endowed with perception and feeling. We—the masters—must therefore reconcile ourselves to the fact that the rebel is out of earshot of our generation. The most we can hope to communicate to him, apart from our professional expertise, is what I have called the technique of successful dissent.

Another difficulty arises from the fact that the rebel is not content to regard the university as a closed society and to live his life inside it. He embarrasses the establishment by his cosmopolitan interests; he is likely to use the machinery of student government to lodge protests over Hungary, over Suez, over Vietnam, over South Africa, over Mississippi. The masters fear that these protests could lead to more serious student participation (I was once prevented from addressing a student audience in an African university because the students had gone on strike in protest against the government). All this involvement of students in outside affairs is exasperating for university administrators; but administrators are paid to be patient. The alternatives are to suppress it or to educate rebels so that they participate in as mature a way as possible. I am sure that only one of these alternatives is consistent with the Athanasian Creed of universities.

Some of these difficulties are of our own making. When scholars came to universities at the age of fourteen, it was proper that masters should be regarded as parent substitutes. But paternalism in universities is now difficult to sustain, and in any case to fuss over boys of eighteen runs counter to the spirit of the age and to the freedom which their contemporaries outside universities enjoy. Thirty years ago we were prepared to trust boys of this age with guns and bombs; it seems hardly reasonable not to trust them today with liberty. Self-discipline there must be, but a minimum of paternalistic discipline. As Clark and Trow (1966) write, one difficulty in the modern university is that the student is at once "a client, a participant, and a ward." Among the submissions from undergraduates to the University Grants Committee, I came across one moving sentence which crystallises student opinion on this matter: "We want to be treated as much like ordinary citizens as possible"—an important message from the scholars to the masters. The rebel scholar does not want to be a privileged citizen. He can be persuaded to participate in the society he has joined, but on his own terms, which are that he be treated as an adult. He has an important contribution to make to the university, but it will be made at its best if it is moderated not by the masters, but by the members of the other significant subculture: the genuine academic. For our part we, the masters, are entitled to say that we will keep him in the society only on our terms, which are that he voluntarily subscribes to the aims of the society and dissents within the limits of self-imposed discipline.

Scholars eventually graduate and go out into the world. Is

this principle of coequality in the university, with all its consequences, consistent with the role of graduates in society? I am convinced that it is. The paradigm of a graduate forty years ago was the conventional person, ready to take responsibility for preserving a set of values which he felt no need to question; deferring to his elders because they were older, not because they were wiser; obedient to principles, constitutions, traditions. That sort of person cannot cope with the modern world. The contemporary paradigm is a person educated for insecurity, who can innovate, improvise, solve problems with no precedent. He must have expert knowledge. That is what he gets from his lectures and laboratories. He must also have the confidence which comes from participation in community living. That is what he gets from belonging, as a coequal, to a society of chancellor, masters, and scholars.

Chapter VI

✿✿✿✿✿✿✿✿✿✿✿✿✿✿✿✿✿✿✿✿✿✿✿✿✿✿✿✿✿✿✿✿

The Academic
Profession

The academic profession is a comparative newcomer to the learned professions. In the nineteenth century many professorships were held part-time by men whose main occupation was a practice in law or medicine or office in the church. The profession therefore lacked identity. This lack of identity has now returned; the modern academic suffers a divided loyalty between the university he serves and the professional guild (of chemists or historians and so on) to which he belongs. This divided loyalty creates ambiguities in the use of academic freedom. The modern academic has a problem also to reconcile the intellectual detachment essential for good scholarship with the social concern essential for the good life.

Some years ago I was present at the centenary celebrations of the Massachusetts Institute of Technology. One of the events was a seminar attended by a score of distinguished scientists. At one point in the seminar, after two European-born, but now American, Nobel prizewinners had spoken, someone said: "You notice that the international language of science is English with a foreign accent."

This remark expresses vividly what English-speaking countries owe to some of the European intellectuals—not only scientists, of course—who were obliged by the storms of history to leave their homelands. I am glad of this opportunity to pay tribute to the contribution they have made to the intellectual life of Britain. Many of them have joined the academic profession and have brought to it the European tradition of academic freedom. It is appropriate, therefore, to reflect on one aspect of this tradition, namely the way university teachers use academic freedom in its narrow personal sense—the sense that is embodied in the word *Lehrfreiheit* (freedom of teaching). But first it is necessary to draw a distinction between the corporate freedom of a university and the academic freedom of teachers in a university. There is a distinction; the concepts are not synonymous. Indeed, a fully autonomous university can nevertheless challenge the academic freedom of its members, as Oxford did when it hauled Benjamin Jowett before the Vice-Chancellor's Court in 1863; and a university which is not autonomous can nevertheless safeguard the academic freedom of its members, as Prussian universities did in Wilhelm von Humboldt's time. My theme is the use made of the personal freedoms within the university which academics expect and which—in Britain and many other countries—they certainly receive.

It is a right of all citizens in this country to say, teach, and publish what they think, subject only to limitations set by the law of the land. Academic freedom does not exceed this right; but it does exempt academics from constraints upon this right, such as are imposed by many other professions. Indeed academic freedom empowers a university teacher to carry this right into the actual discharge of his contract with the institution he serves. Within the easy constraints set by a faculty board or the head of a department (and even these constraints are arguable) he fulfils his contract by devising his own teaching programme and choosing his own research projects; and outside his contract he can promulgate his views— whether or not they lie within his expertise—without endangering his job. He can, with impunity, upset the theories of his professor by his research, and embarrass the vice-chancellor by his letters to *The Times*. This is a greater degree of freedom than is allowed to men belonging to other institutions, such as the civil service, the army, or the priesthood of the Roman Catholic church. How is it that the academic profession has acquired these privileges?

The privileges have their origin in history and their support in the style of nineteenth-century English society (and it is one of our contemporary problems that this style has changed). The colleges of Oxford and Cambridge were wealthy enough to preserve a great deal of freedom from the State and—in their more vigorous phases—even from the Church. They used this freedom to preserve the medieval concept of the university as a guild of masters, each master (in the modern jargon of the left) "doing his own thing." And the style of nineteenth-century English society was to leave higher education to private enterprise, to respect the autonomy of private corporations, to recognize that the profession of teaching was best pursued with a minimum of restraint from Church or State.

I say "profession," but compared with the professions of medicine, law, and the Church, the academic profession is—in modern times—a comparative newcomer. Census analyses in the nineteenth century, and indeed up to 1911, distinguished a score of professional occupations, which included actors, midwives, and surveyors, but which lumped the academic profession into the category of "teachers." It seems at first strange that a profession which even a century ago was making claims on the indulgence of society for special freedoms should have had so little identity; but the reason is, I think, simple. In the early nineteenth century, before the rise of the civic universities, the only prestigious teaching posts in England were in Oxford and Cambridge; and in these two universities practically all the teaching was done by colleges. Up to about ninety years ago the colleges required their Fellows to be celibate. Therefore, except for the chronic bachelor, a Fellowship was not a first step on the academic ladder; it was an interlude which had to lead, on marriage, to some other profession: a church living or a post in a public school. It was one of the grievances laid before the Royal Commissioners on Cambridge in 1852 that college teaching was "only a temporary employment during a few years of early life, and not a definite and acknowledged career." In England (though not in Scotland), even for professors, a chair was not a career post. No less a person than Henry Maine, in giving evidence before the Cambridge Commissioners on his own Chair of Civil Law, said: "It is virtually impossible that any Professor should make the conduct and regulation of his Faculty the principal occupation of his life. I myself am a practising barrister—my two immediate predecessors were beneficed clergymen." And John S. Henslow, professor of botany in Cambridge, was unable to suggest any improvements in the duties of his Chair, "consistent with my duties to my parish" (*Report of H. M. Commissioners Appointed to Inquire into the State, Discipline, Studies, and Revenues of the University and Colleges of Cambridge,* 1852–1853). In the Oxford of 1852 it was no better; the Royal Commission there wrote of the desirability for a university professorship to become "a recognised profession" (*Report of H. M. Commissioners Appointed to Inquire into the State, Discipline, Studies, and Revenues of the University and Colleges of Oxford,* 1852). In short, the chronic weakness of the academic profession at that time was a divided loyalty; part of my theme is that this divided loyalty has now returned in another form.

If academic freedom was not often questioned in nineteenth-century England, it was because no one cared much what professors taught or wrote; academic freedom was of little concern. And the concomitants of academic freedom—security in the profession and control of its standards—were correspondingly ill defined outside the ancient universities. For example, at Manchester until 1870 professors were frankly employees of the Board of Trustees, although (in deference to the traditions in Oxford and Cambridge) the Trustees delegated academic business to the principal and the professors. But academic freedom was not always granted so liberally: professors in some new universities, for example Sonnenschein in Birmingham, had to fight for control of academic business. As recently as 1910, when the Haldane Commission was reviewing the constitution of the

University of London, the Vice-Chancellor said in his evidence that he "hoped the Commission would pronounce in favour of teachers being represented on the Governing Body" of schools of the university; and he salted his plea with the anecdote that at a meeting of the Council of University College, before it included any academic representatives, he heard one member of the council say to another: "When a professor walks into the council room, I shall walk out" (Royal Commission on University Education in London, appendix to third report, 1911).

But the lack of identity and cohesion in the academic profession has, I believe, deeper causes than divided loyalty. There has been and still is an uncertainty about the uses of academic freedom. Perhaps the cause of this uncertainty is that in this country the fight for the concomitants of academic freedom—security of tenure and control of standards—was won half a century ago; but the uses to which academic freedom should be put have not been defined. I think that in the future this freedom may be challenged; therefore it is worthwhile to examine how academic freedom has been used over the last century, how it is being used today, and how it ought to be used tomorrow.

There is one clear use of academic freedom which has not changed over the last century, namely the practice of publishing new ideas and new discoveries, not only without fear of suppression because they challenge orthodoxy, but also with the assurance that if the ideas and discoveries stand up to criticism, they will become the new orthodoxy and will displace the old. In the world of research there is no class hierarchy; pundits have no permanent standing, and the whole fabric of learning is held together by a consensus of what constitutes sound scholarship. In this respect the academic profession does seem to have established unwritten, supra-national, professional standards, which are independent of nationality, race, politics, and religion.

But research and scholarship are not the only duties expected of the academic profession. Indeed as duties they are comparatively recent. Even in Scotland, which had a well-established professoriate, it was asserted, in evidence before the Royal Commission of 1876, that "the Scotch professor does not yet consider research to be one of his duties" (*Report of the Royal Commission Appointed to Inquire into the Universities of Scotland,* 1878). Haldane, in another Royal Commission a generation later, was still having to emphasise that research was part of a professor's duty. This duty, however, should not obscure the fact that the primary responsibility of a profession of university teachers is to teach in universities. And it is in the use of academic freedom in the discharge of this responsibility that one finds, over the last hundred years, a certain ambivalence.

To suggest to university teachers that university teaching is their prime responsibility is to stir a curious resentment among some of them. So let me assert at once that the academic profession in Britain is probably more dedicated to teaching, and more successful in its dedication, than are academics in universities anywhere else. Our students do receive personal attention from senior professors; care is paid to their individual needs; anxious thought is devoted to admitting, teaching, and examining them; (to say nothing of the writing of scores of references afterwards)—all this to a degree which I believe is not equalled in America or Russia or on the continent of Europe. And, as one byproduct, British universities have the lowest "drop-out" rate of any in the world.

But, granted all this, there is a curious gap in the attitude of the profession to that part of its duty which concerns teaching. The profession neither demands nor provides for any training or internship for the activity which is its prime responsibility; and it has no explicit code of conduct towards those whom it serves—its students—as the doctor has towards his patient, the lawyer towards his client, the banker towards his customer. The consequence of this is that different members of the profession regard this part of their responsibility in very diverse ways. Academic freedom permits this diversity. Diversity is almost always to be preferred to uniformity. But the drawback of this diversity is, I maintain, a lack of "cohesion of intent" in the academic profession, such as is not found among, for example, medical practitioners or barristers.

In Britain, up to the First World War, the paradigm of a university teacher—at any rate in the humanities—was not the research-centred German professor; it was the reformed Oxbridge college don whose aim (as Mark Pattison put it) was to produce "not a book but a man." The curriculum—classics, history, or philosophy—was taught rigorously and with a very high standard.

But these subjects were commonly regarded as tools to sharpen the mind, rather than as ends in themselves. This was one expression of the use of academic freedom in teaching the young. The freedom was used to fashion a man in a certain tradition, to tailor him to a certain style of intellectual life, even to persuade him to adopt a certain pattern of conformity. Now the emphasis has changed. Butterfield (1962) illustrated this change when he said that in his young days, when the Faculty Board of History at Cambridge discussed questions of syllabus, the board members spoke in their capacity as supervisors, interested in the whole intellectual development of the young men in their charge. Nowadays, he went on to say, "when we are discussing the syllabus, I believe we tend to speak rather as University Lecturers, each of us a little more concerned to look after the fortunes of his own branch of the study." From the United States a similar contrast can be drawn. In 1915 the American Association of University Professors published a *Declaration of Principles* which included the sentence: "It is not only the character of the instruction but also the character of the instructor that counts; and if the student has reason to believe that the instructor is not true to himself, the virtue of the instruction as an educative force is incalculably diminished." When, in 1966, the association issued a *Statement on Professional Ethics,* the emphasis on "the character of the instructor" had vanished.

I am not concerned to criticise this attitude; I mention it to illustrate that over the last fifty years there has been an unplanned change in the intent of the academic profession towards its teaching duties: many academics use academic freedom in their teaching differently from the way their predecessors used it two generations ago.

In American universities this preoccupation with the subject rather than with the student has been carried to such extremes that there is genuine and justified alarm about "the flight from teaching." There are universities in America which attract star professors by assuring them that they need not be on the campus for more than one year in three. The flight from teaching is not due to laziness— these jet-set professors work very hard—but to the extraneous calls to which the successful academic is now expected to respond: university boards, editing a learned journal, the mail (most of it not concerned with university work at all), invitations to sit on government committees or on the council of a professional society. The temptations are there, and academic freedom strips the teacher of protection against them. This has led one American professor, Jacques Barzun (1968), to assert that some modern academics in America ("scholars in orbit" he calls them) now redefine academic freedom as the freedom to choose what they shall do and when, and to withhold any service they please.

In Britain it would be untrue to say there has been a flight from teaching. There is abundant evidence to the contrary. And the slick complaint—that the duties of teaching and research are irreconcilable—is belied by the achievements of thousands of university teachers in Britain. But these are not grounds for complacency. Let me support this assertion by an illustration.

There is no doubt that the academic profession has again become a profession of divided loyalties; not for the reasons which made it so in the nineteenth century, but because the academic finds that the claims of the guild of university teachers, demanding loyalty to the university he serves and the pupils under his care, can easily be overshadowed by the claims of a second guild to which he belongs: that of his peers in his specialism. Ask yourselves which judgment matters most to a young physicist: the judgement of the vice-chancellor and senate and students of his own university, or the judgement of physicists in the Royal Society and on the committees which distribute grants from the Science Research Council? There is a broad overlap in the criteria for earning golden opinions from both sources; but the criteria are not identical. And there is a temptation, on the lower steps of the academic ladder, to allocate less time than one would like to the art of teaching and to leisurely talking with undergraduates, and more time to what is ironically described as "my own work." If "my own work" were always directly relevant to the teaching which has to be done, there would still be no clash between the two activities. But the motive to do research is not always the need to improve the quality of one's teaching, nor is it always an irrepressible desire to discover new facts or ideas. Sometimes, in science at any rate, the motive is little more than the need to publish papers in order to secure recognition and promotion. This pressure to publish is not new, but it is more noticeable nowadays because of the age structure in the profession. In a stable profession there is an even spread of age, from early twenties to early sixties. But universities which have expanded quickly find that they have about five times as many teachers in the thirty to thirty-five age group as in the fifty to fifty-five age group. It is on these young academics that the pressure operates.

At the top of the academic ladder a new challenge to loyalty appears: the call to professors to serve on the committees of research councils, learned societies, and government departments. This claim upon their time is necessary and important for the whole academic world. If the University Grants Committee and the research councils and their committees were not manned by men like these, the autonomy of learning and even academic freedom itself would be endangered. They are the insulation between the scholar and the state. But these activities do contribute to a division of loyalties in the academic profession.

Research and service on committees are unpaid; but a third temptation to the use of academic freedom is the paid consultancy. The present-day academic, in some subjects, finds that he has a highly marketable skill. The tradition of academic freedom permits him to put his skill on the market, notwithstanding the fact that he has a fulltime job as a university teacher. Sometimes he is right to do so, but the profession provides no criteria by which he can judge whether or not he is right.

So it is a dilemma. On the one hand universities are faced with a massive increase in student numbers, and the obligation to teach will not diminish; it will increase. On the other hand the emphasis on the prime responsibility of the academic profession is shifting from being student-centred (though this remains, in Britain, an important element) to being subject-centred, or (for some senior members of the profession) to serving as a scholar statesman. The pace of advancement in knowledge has made research in many fields competitive instead of contemplative, and for some scholars this has distorted the purpose of research. Furthermore, the need for scholar-statesmen makes it essential that some scholars, at any rate, devote some of their time to committees and to advising governments. The problem cannot be solved simply by directives to academics on how to divide their time among these competing demands. It is part of academic freedom that they have to make this choice themselves. The choice therefore becomes a problem in how to use academic freedom. The American Association of University Professors clearly recognises this, as its *Statement on Professional Ethics* (1966) points out: "[The professor] determines the amount and character of the work he does outside his institution with due regard to his paramount interests within it." But the statement offers no guidance on how "due regard" is to be measured.

In 1963 an attempt at guidance was made by a government committee in Britain, the National Board for Prices and Incomes, in a report on salaries of university teachers. The report tried, albeit in a clumsy and tactless way, to establish two things: to define the academic profession and to distinguish it from other professions; and to specify the purpose of the profession and the balance to be expected from its practitioners between teaching, research, and extramural activities.

These intentions were important and timely, but they failed. It is not my purpose here to analyse the failure. Suffice it to say that first, the report perpetuated differential salary scales between university teachers in medicine and other university teachers (instead of recommending some pattern of dual university and hospital appointments with separate sources of salary), and this severely damaged the concept that university teaching is a distinguishable profession with separate scales of pecuniary rewards, where emolument is based on distinction within the profession (whether in medicine or Sanskrit) and not on competition from another quite different profession. Second, the report, while very properly advocating that a profession of university teachers should offer inducements for good teaching, destroys its advocacy by the assumption that the ideas of productivity can be applied to the art of teaching. University teachers create in their pupils, as artists do on their canvasses and poets with their pens, qualities which cannot be properly evaluated until years afterwards, and which vary from masterpieces (think of the pupils of Rutherford and Namier) to mediocrity. The concepts of productivity, disengaged from quality, are simply irrelevant to these operations. Apply the concepts of cost effectiveness by all means to buildings, administration, catering, residence, and even to a rationalisation of which universities should teach which subjects; but, applied to the art of teaching and the production of graduates, the concept is nonsense. It is the new breach of trust to imagine that a university should be satisfied simply to achieve the most efficient movement in a direction planned for it. On the contrary, its object is to scrutinise all the time the appropriateness of the direction planned. This activity cannot be evaluated by cost accountants. It is valid for teaching even more than it is for research because teaching is inevitably manipulating the lives of others. The statement in the report: "We consider how best the levels and structure of university salaries should be altered with a view to promoting lower costs per student at a difficult moment for the economy," will go down in history as one of the more philistine remarks made by a British government agency; the most stupid way to lower costs would be to relate the salary structure of the profession to the output of graduates, without regard to the quality of the output.

But this is a digression. My theme is the uses of academic freedom, and I digressed in order to say that the Prices and Incomes Board tried to clarify these uses, and failed. But we do well not to disregard its reminder that the prime responsibility of a university teacher is to diminish ignorance, both his own ignorance and that of his pupils. Diminishing the ignorance of one's pupils is an art, improved by training; and it is a different training from that needed for diminishing one's own ignorance. University teachers are very well trained to diminish their own ignorance, and they set great store by this training. It is surely an indictment of the profession that its members do not require from themselves any training or internship in the art of diminishing the ignorance of their pupils.

But we have not done with the argument yet. Diminish the ignorance of one's pupils, but in which areas? Here we encounter what is, in my view, the most perplexing problem in the uses of academic freedom. The prime duty of a university teacher is to diminish ignorance in the area of his own specialism: biophysics, Tudor history, medieval French. But, traditionally, university teaching has meant much more than that. Indeed in the minds of many academics it still does. A few years ago groups of university teachers submitted memoranda for visitations by the University Grants Committee. This statement came from one university: "We feel very strongly that the university should contribute to the development of its students in much more than a strictly subject- or profession-oriented way." And this from another: "We favour an increase in numbers of halls of residence 'where tutorial care and the education of the whole man are held to be essential features.' " These statements urge that university teaching include more than academic instruction, and that teachers use academic freedom for pastoral as well as for narrowly professional purposes; indeed, that they include a moral content in university education. If there is to be a code of conduct in the academic profession towards those whom it serves, analogous to the codes in other professions, university teachers need to decide where they stand on this question.

Some university teachers are already sure where they stand. A university, they say, is not an institution for moral training. It is not even a place dedicated to wisdom, only to knowledge. A university will, Moberly (1949) wrote, teach students how to make bombs or cathedrals, but it will not teach them which of these objects they ought to make. The typical nineteenth-century don believed that what he taught should be not only accurate but edifying; today some of his successors believe that all that is required of their teaching is disinterested accuracy. The only rules these teachers would enforce on the academic community are those essential to preserve it as a place of learning and research. On the social implications of knowledge, even more on manners, ethics, and lifestyle, they adopt a policy of nonintervention.

Academic freedom permits the university teacher to adopt this attitude, and there are arguments in its favour: it keeps the university out of politics and helps to preserve its autonomy. But to take this attitude is to withdraw from a responsibility which has been traditionally accepted by dons in Britain. If it were to become the accepted code of conduct in the academic profession, it could reduce the teacher-student relationship to one in which the teacher was simply selling knowledge and technique—a relationship which might become as impersonal as the relationship between a customer and his grocer. And, paradoxically, this impersonal relationship is one which students reject.

This paradox is relevant to my theme. When one sorts out the motives behind student unrest (putting aside the shrill cult of nihilism and the doctrinaire demands for "student power" which assume falsely that a university is a mini-state and not a guild of masters and apprentices; the hypocrisy, for hypocrisy is no monopoly of my generation, which claims the rights but rejects the responsibilities of studentship; and the mere mischief-making of "protest-for-kicks") one discovers among some thoughtful students one motive which we do well to respect: a demand that there should be a moral value in higher education. But it is a paradoxical demand, as though the student were repeating Pattison's formula, "Not a book but a man," and adding, "but not a man like *you*." Among the graffiti written on the walls of the university at Nanterre was a cynical adaptation of Descartes: "*They* think: therefore I am." This expresses a confession and resentment that university teachers do influence their pupils. Some pupils resist having to accept from their teachers a style of life and a set of assumptions and value judgements about society, as a package deal thrown in with their academic work. They fear that they will imbibe from the professor of chemistry not only chemistry but also what they regard as his compromise with a corrupt world which prostitutes science. And yet—and this is the paradox—these same pupils are asking their teachers to reconcile, somehow, the intellectual detachment essential for good scholarship with the social concern essential for the good life; to establish, as Frye (1967) puts it, "the human context into which knowledge fits . . . What we have to determine is to what extent concern is a scholarly virtue, and whether or not it is, like detachment, a precondition of knowledge." One pamphlet, aptly called a "Black Paper," put out by earnest men who are alarmed by what they call a "progressive collapse" in British education, sneers at the student demonstrators in one of the new universities who said that they wished to be taught "life" instead of literature, history, or science. But perhaps these students are saying, with the ignorance, brashness, and arrogance of youth, that they want university education to have a moral value. And did not Jowett, Sedgwick, Seeley, and other great teachers do just what the students ask: teach the art of living, using as tools classics, geology, and history? When students ask for "relevance" we have to criticise and sometimes reject their demands, for by relevance many of them mean an intellectual parochialism, a concentration on topics and not on disciplines. But when they ask for guidance in how to relate their studies to their

own moral and social value judgements, they are asking for something which they will need in any career or profession. A score of
times each year I am asked by students: "What am I being taught
English or engineering *for?*" Most students, still, can answer this
question for themselves. But some genuinely want guidance. Can it
be given without dogma and without hypocrisy? I believe it can,
not by indoctrinating students with a repertoire of moral principles
—that way danger lies—but by asserting that the discipline of
scholarship carries its own ethical values: reverence for truth, with
the recognition, which generates humility, that all truth may be con-
taminated by error; equality, for any scholar, however junior, who
advances knowledge has his place in the guild of learning; interna-
tionalism, for it is immaterial whether a scholar's theory is upset by
one of his countrymen or by an enemy, by a black man or a yellow
man, by a Christian or a Muslim—the theory is upset all the same.
Moral authority in universities, therefore, can be an authority which
avoids dogma and which lays down the pragmatic conditions under
which scholarship can be pursued. And what is valid for scholarship
is valid for all rational decision-making. Arrogance, insincerity, prejudice, intolerance, failure to ascertain the facts: these are incom-
patible with intellectual health, whether in research, politics, or
commerce.

There is a need for the academic profession to define its
complex loyalties more clearly; and the definition, which already
covers adequately the duty of the university teacher towards his subject, should also clarify the duty of the university teacher towards his
pupils. The arguable question is whether this duty includes the teaching of concern as well as detachment. I think it does. The protesting
student who is worth listening to is the one who wants the academic
profession to offer a pattern of leadership, authority, and example
which he can accept. In its standards of scholarship, in the expertise
of its practitioners, the profession does this already. We have to be
uncompromising about the virtues of detachment in scholarship. We
have to insist that issues must be resolved by reason and persuasion,
not by disruption or force. We must have no patience with those
who choose to come to universities, and yet who profess to despise
the intellectual approach, who reject objectivity and discipline, and
who replace these qualities with vague emotional commitment. But

more than this is required of us. We must reassure the young that intellectual detachment is not inconsistent with social concern, for social concern unites large numbers of students—many more than those who demonstrate—with the rest of their generation. They will not break this tie. If these students do not learn from their teachers that the academic tradition can coexist with concern for society, they will reject the academic tradition. The threat to the present generation comes not so much from us but from themselves, for some of the protesting young reject experience. Experience, in their view, spells compromise with the powers of evil. They are, therefore, rejecting what they themselves will become in ten years' time. I think it is a duty of university teachers to save them from this tragic misjudgement. It will not be easy; the world is changing so fast that, for the first time in history, I suppose, it is arguable whether experience can keep pace with the need for adaptation.

But we who belong to the academic profession should (in my view) regard the solution to this problem as our duty. What really unites members of the academic profession is not an interest in one another's scholarship but our common participation in the mechanism of intellectual heredity: we are the analogues of chromosomes in physical heredity. Our duty is to perpetuate the stability of tradition coupled with the potential for changing tradition, to transmit orthodoxy coupled with a technique for constructive dissent from orthodoxy. This is a prime use of academic freedom.

Chapter VII

✿✿✿✿✿✿✿✿✿✿✿✿✿✿✿✿✿✿✿✿✿✿✿✿✿✿✿✿✿✿

The Scientist as
University President

The heavy social responsibilities on universities today put strain on the long-time pattern of university government and the role of university administrators. Accordingly, administrators must often grope their way in darkness toward the principles of their profession. Scientific training can in some ways prove useful to the administrator—if it does not incapacitate him from making decisions, realizing that they are exercises in probability.

Over forty years ago I was a graduate student at the University of Chicago. One day, soon after I arrived there from England, I was eating lunch at the Quadrangle Club. A tall, rugged man, with hair brushed back, came to sit at my table. He was many years my senior but we slipped easily into conversation. I do not remember what we discussed except that it included water polo and the differences between American and British rules of play. What I do remember vividly is that there was a disciplined enthusiasm about him, an inner tranquillity, a natural friendliness, a mixture of gaiety and gravity which immensely impressed me. I did not know the man's name. I discovered afterwards he was Arthur Compton.

I have only a layman's understanding of the massive contributions which Compton made to physics and I am not competent to comment on his place in science. But I must confess that for me the most impressive episode of his career was his decision in 1945 to give up science for academic administration. There is an element of sacrifice, and some risk, when a scientist of such eminence changes the patterns of thought of a lifetime to become a university president.

But do the patterns of thought change? What precisely is the expertise of university administration? Is science a good training for the university presidency? And how should the faculty regard university administrators? These are questions I invite you to consider.

When I left scientific work to become a university president, after having been a professor for thirteen years, someone gave me this advice: "Remember that in the eyes of professors all administrators are an evil. Say to yourself every morning: 'I am an evil: am I a necessary one?' " I took his advice; I have often asked myself that question. My answers are based on my experience of the status of university administrators in Britain, but things may not be very different in America. It is only a generation ago that an American, Thorstein Veblen (1957), published a savage indictment against university presidents and called them "captains of erudition." I would not be surprised to find faculty members in the United States who share Veblen's distaste for academic administrators and reluctantly accept them as a necessary evil.

How have academic administrators—these apparent parasites on honest endeavor—come into being? Let us start with some axioms and assumptions. Both in the United States and Britain we are dedicated to the belief that people are individuals with free will and choice. We observe that they attach themselves to groups, communities, and institutions. The purpose of their attachment is cooperation. They can choose, within limits, which units of society they will join. They still retain a personal and private life apart from the group, and in this area they continue to make decisions which are their personal and private affair. But in joining a unit of society they agree to allow some decisions to be made for them by the group. This is true of small units of society, like a club or a college, and it is true of large units of society like an industry or the army. In some groups individuals surrender all participation in the making of certain decisions; in others they take part in decision-making by the group.

Even in small units of society, decision-making can be difficult; as anyone knows who has driven a family into the country and the family has had to decide where to stop for a picnic. In large units of society, where the purposes of cooperation may be hard to define, decision-making becomes extremely difficult. It is a matter of observation that when decision-making becomes difficult one of two things is likely to happen: either the group fails to make a decision, in which case cooperation—the purpose of the group—disintegrates and the group disperses; or someone in the group assumes leadership, concentrates and clarifies opinion, and, as it were, precipitates out a decision. If he is skilled in exercising leadership, cooperation improves and the purpose of the group is fulfilled; and he may find himself repeatedly called upon to crystallise decisions on behalf of the group. If he is not skilled, the group disintegrates or seeks another leader.

Such is the origin of the administrator. He is someone who precipitates out decisions on behalf of units of society. Just now I attached to him that very inflammable word "leader;" but observe one very important thing about him which is often overlooked. He has what appears to be authority and power, and he may enjoy prestige and privilege; but in fact the key to authority and power is held by all members of the group. He administers because—and only because—the group is content to abide by his decisions. Even if he holds his leadership by force rather than consent, even if his orders are backed by a gun, nevertheless he will not last long unless the group either cooperates with him or at least acquiesces to his policy. In brief, the art of using authority is to secure consent. The good administrator is not a boss but a persuader.

No one is likely to dispute the importance of administrators for decision-making in such institutions as armies, industries, and jails. And no one is likely to dispute the utter irrelevance of administrators for decision-making in personal affairs like marriage (though this *is* a matter for administrative decision in some African societies) and in the creative arts. When we come to science and scholarship the question is not so easy to answer. In the strategy of research the decisions which matter are personal decisions made by the individual worker: whether to design this experiment or that, whether to pursue this interpretation or that, whether to teach this part of the subject or another part. In a sense, the purpose of a university is best served if its policy decisions are based upon the personal decisions of the faculty. Creative artists still manage to remain outside the mesh of red tape which encircles the civilized world. So, until about a century ago, did scientists and scholars. But the world of science and scholarship is now heavily infested with administrators. I believe this is inevitable and that administrators are necessary; but the administration of science and scholarship is a new branch of the profession requiring new techniques. It is not sufficient to apply, without any adaptation, the traditional techniques of administration to be found in the army or in the Church or in government.

The case for administrators in science and scholarship is simple to establish. It arises simply from the size and diversity of the groups necessary to support these activities. Robert Boyle and Charles Darwin were able to do their work without having to secure the consent or even acquiescence of large numbers of people. When Boyle wanted to make a new piece of apparatus or Darwin wanted to build a new shed in his garden, their desires did not have to be set against the rival claims of other scientists for apparatus and buildings. There are still a few corners of science and scholarship which can be cultivated in this way; but the vast majority of people who want to do research or pursue learning now must join a unit of society organized for this purpose. Their wishes cannot be fulfilled without impinging on the wishes of others; they have to practise cooperation;

and on some decisions they must be willing to consent to authority. In a word, they must put up with administrators. When this change first came over science and scholarship the problems of administration were simple: the groups were small and informal; the administrators were parttime amateurs, little more than spokesmen for their colleagues. In the University of Melbourne in Australia, for instance, there was no fulltime university president until 1933. The professors ran the university in their spare time. Those easy days are over. British universities now spend about sixty million dollars a month, and 90 percent of this money comes from public funds. Expenditure in American universities is astronomically higher than this. Universities and research institutes would grind to a halt without professional administrators. They act as channels of communication between the higher learning and society. On one hand they mobilize and transmit public support for higher learning; on the other hand they interpret the university to the people who support it. To keep these channels open and fresh is nowadays a challenge to any man, even a man of the stature of Arthur Compton.

One would think that a profession as important as the administration of higher learning would surely have some principles to guide its practitioners, but remarkably little has been written about university administration. Textbooks on industrial management or public administration—there are plenty of these—do not help much, for they make one basic assumption which is repugnant to the whole spirit of science and scholarship, namely that policy originates at the top and travels downwards. For all but certain kinds of applied research, policy originates at the bench, in the laboratory, in the library, and round the lunch table, and percolates upwards and outwards. In the army, in government, and in industry, a big overall decision at the top generates a wave of subdecisions running out into the remotest channels and creeks of the organization: to the private soldier, the stenographer, the truck driver. In organizations concerned with science and scholarship, however, there are foci of decision-making all over the organization, and these decisions must somehow be coordinated—and coordinated in such a way that members of the organization suffer the minimum of restraint—if the integrity of the organization is to be preserved.

Because there has been very little analysis of this sort of organization, administrators of higher learning have to grope their way in darkness toward the principles of their profession. Let us join them in this groping by watching the academic administrator at work. I choose an administrator from Britain because I am more familiar with his habits, but I believe this summary of observations would be valid, with some modifications, for his counterpart elsewhere.

A university is a society of scholars who agree to cooperate to effectively advance and transmit knowledge. The chief administrator in all but two British universities (Oxford and Cambridge) is a permanent official, the principal or vice-chancellor. He corresponds to the American university president. His function is to promote the purpose of the university. He cannot directly help scholars teach or do research; in all but one of the subjects of the curriculum he probably knows less than the youngest assistant, and in his one subject of expertise he is likely soon to become hopelessly out of date. What then can he do to promote the purpose of the university?

Let us watch him at work. The University of Middletown is preparing its quinquennial plan for the University Grants Committee. In order to qualify for a grant, the University must specify the buildings, equipment, and staff it requires, and it must cost it all as accurately as possible. The task of preparing the plan is entrusted to a committee consisting of the president (who took classics at Oxford), the honorary treasurer (who is an accountant in the city), and the deans of the faculties of arts, science, and medicine: a historian, a geologist, and a paediatrician. They are not fulltime deans; they are professors appointed for periods of two years to do this work parttime. These constitute a syndicate of administrators who have to make decisions of far-reaching importance. Of course, their decisions are made after prolonged consultation with faculty boards and departments and must be discussed and endorsed by the University senate and council. There will be a lot of dissent, but it is unlikely that further thinking will be contributed to the work after it leaves the committee. On this committee the president is the only man who has a grasp of the problem as a whole: he knows how high the bids can be before they become unrealistic, what projects are likely to get support from industry, how cooperative the city is likely to be over the acquisition of sites, and so on. So he carries a correspondingly heavy share of responsibility for the decisions.

Let us now consider one single item in the quinquennial plan,

The University has one unallocated site across the London road. Before the committee there are four applications for this site: The professor of biology, in twenty foolscap pages of single-spaced type-script, presses rather querulously the need for a new building; biology is the Cinderella of the faculty, he says, and the whole future of his research school depends on a new building. The librarian, in two lucid and persuasive pages, asks for a science library on this site; shelf space in the stacks, he says, is sufficient for only four more years and the library is the core of the University on which even the scientists depend. The refectory committee press strongly for a new cafeteria on the site; pointing out acidly that there is a half-hour queue every lunch hour, that the University has committed itself publicly to an increase of 75 percent, and that it will be scandalous not to have adequate catering arrangements. The faculty of engineer-ing, in half a page, put up a confident—not to say arrogant—claim for a new institute of aerodynamics on the site. They support their claim by offering to devote a recent bequest to defraying the cost of equipping the new building (it would in fact defray only a third of the cost), and they end with a hint that there will be political trou-ble is they have no adequate arrangements for aerodynamics.

Five men, none of whom is an expert on biology or libraries or cafeterias or engineering, must decide what is to be built on this site; and the decision has to be made within a limited time. What is the process of decision-making? It is clearly of a different order from decision-making in scientific research or scholarship. One difference is that there is a time factor, which can be neglected in science but which cannot be neglected here: there must be a decision on the use of the site, whether there are enough data for the decision or not. Another difference is that once the decision is acted upon there can be no going back, whereas if a scientist makes a wrong decision about a research problem he can return to his starting point—half a dozen times if necessary. A third difference is that no one could ever reach a decision on this question solely by logical processes. The president will doubtless provide a pseudo-logical rationalization afterwards to make the decision respectable and to attempt to pacify the losers; but in fact the decision itself will have to be made through an extrapolation beyond logic. It is common knowledge among ad-ministrators that if a man relies on reason alone in such circumstances he ends up in a sticky morass of hesitation, fear, and lack of initiative. Nothing is decided.

But the process of decision can begin logically. There is a sort of Ohm's law in decision-making: Standing in the way of fulfilment of all decisions there are resistances; if these resistances are too great, action cannot flow and the decision, even if made, is not viable. An administrator who makes nonviable decisions is a failure. So the committee must familiarize itself with the resistances. If a cafeteria is built on the site, thousands of students will be crossing a main road between 12:30 and 1:00 every day. Does this disqualify the cafeteria? If aerodynamics is put there it will be isolated from the engineering precinct, where there might be (but there is no assurance on this) another site available in five years' time. If a library is put on the site it would have to be ten floors high: will planning permission be given for so tall a building? And a biology department on the site would suffer from vibration and noise from the road, which would interfere with some of the equipment.

Most likely, none of these resistances totally disqualifies any of the proposals. The result of the application of Ohm's law in administration is that while there are resistances to all solutions, none of the resistances entirely eliminates any of the solutions. The committee then have to go beyond logic. They must first of all carefully try to eliminate any prejudice due to personalities: the querulous biology professor, the plausible librarian, the testy refectory committee, or the arrogant engineering dean. (Perhaps at this point I should say what is said on the first page of novels: every faculty member mentioned here is purely fictitious.) Then comes the extrapolation from logic. In solving a problem like this the committee simply cannot use the technique Darwin tried before he decided to get married: jot down a list of pros and cons and add them up. They have to get in their minds a picture of the university as a whole as an architect has in mind his building as a whole, and by the exercise of a nonlogical process—call it intuition, judgment, perception, or what you will—they have to fit first one solution and then another into the picture and decide which (to use an Americanism) is the most "purposeful"—I prefer to risk saying "the most aesthetically satisfying"—for the university as a whole.

Of course the decision is not made merely by contemplating,

in a Yoga-like state of relaxation, the needs of the university. The president and possibly his associates on the committee consult departments, architects, city planners, the University Grants Committee, and colleagues in other universities. He has to go on doing this until the situation as a whole is developed like an image on a photographic plate in his mind. It is an exhausting process, and clarity, if it comes at all, will be followed by a noticeable degree of emotional exhaustion. One thing is certain: after eliminating any solution which is impossible or impracticable, the committee will rely on "hunch," although afterwards the president will cover the committee's tracks with a lucid memorandum weighing one proposal against the other and explaining logically how the decision was made. And the outcome? If the resistances are too great or the president too conciliatory, nothing may be built on the site, for during the delay building costs rise, and the pressure for car parks overrides other priorities.

To a scientist accustomed to the austere logic of research, this may seem a dangerously imprecise way to reach a major decision; but even the most distinguished of scientists recognizes the validity of nonlogical approach, provided of course that it is supported by logic as well. Hear what the French mathematician Laplace (1951) says: "The principal means of arriving at truth are: induction, analogy, hypothesis founded upon facts and rectified continually by new observations, and a happy tact given by nature and strengthened by experience." "A happy tact" plays an essential part in major administrative decisions.

At this point no one is ever to know whether a decision finally taken was the wisest, since there is no way to judge between alternatives when only one is tried. I can assure you that history soon enough discloses whether a decision was wise or not, and an administrator's unwise decisions are chalked up against him with ruthless inevitability, often with savage injustice. And as for inadequate evidence for making the decision: are not all major personal decisions made on evidence just as inadequate? Marriage, choice of a career, change of job, a decision to sell shares in a copper mine and to buy shares in a steel mill: to make decisions in areas of ignorance is in fact an exercise in probability. When it is a once for all decision (like marriage) there isn't an opportunity for experience to accumulate, but when decisions in areas of ignorance are made every day (as administrators must make them) experience does accumulate and skill develops; one can cultivate the art of weighing probabilities in areas of ignorance. Just as the power of logical thinking varies enormously among people, so this power of perception and discrimination between what is relevant and what is not— this art of nonlogical judgment—this, too, varies enormously among people, and a successful administrator must have a good measure of both. He takes advice, he consults experts, he uses all data which can be assembled through logical inquiry; but when he has done all this the equation still contains too many unknowns for any deductive solution. His success in decision-making does not depend on his vast and exact knowledge but on his skill at navigating areas of ignorance. In the words of the English poet, Robert Bridges: "wisdom lies in masterful administration of the unforeseen."

The function of the chief administrator in a university is to ensure that the decisions which are made preserve the cohesion of the institution, are consistent with purpose, and contribute to integrity. To fulfil this function he must think in terms of balance and perspective. The professor of biology may be a Nobel prizewinner, but the distinction of his research school will not compensate for a weak library or squalid catering arrangements for students or a badly equipped engineering faculty. A good president regards it as his prime duty to stock the university with experts all of whom constantly have new ideas and are constantly pressing for more money, more accommodation, and more staff. The more enterprising they are, the greater the centrifugal pull on the administration. The art is to keep the institution in balance. In any healthly institution innovation and enthusiasm outrun resources and there arises a succession of conflicts. The purpose of the institution is cooperation, but vitality depends on conflicts. The administrator's duty is not to suppress conflicts; he must encourage them, and when they arise, he must take steps to resolve them. A healthy university, therefore, ought to be in a state of unstable equilibrium, an equilibrium continually disturbed by forces and enthusiasms generated within the faculty, and continually readjusted by the gyroscope of the administration. The power behind the gyroscope is the president. Of course he does not restore equilibrium all by himself. He is surrounded by committees and advisers; but responsibility for bringing the gyroscope into action rests squarely upon his shoulders.

In the United States a good deal of attention has been given recently to the functions of college presidents. The president emeritus of Princeton wrote a book on the subject; a distinguished management consultant made a study of university government; and some years ago Robert Maynard Hutchins delivered an eloquent lecture on the dilemma of university administration. These analyses are not valid on both sides of the Atlantic without modification. If I were writing a handbook for university presidents in Britain, I would consider these four points essential.

First, *administrators must administer.* This seems a superfluous thing to say, but it isn't. When there is a rigid hierarchy of authority, administrators have no alternative but to administer. If a naval captain doesn't make decisions the group under his control collapses. But in an organization like a university where decision-making and authority are so diffused, the administrator is under a great temptation not to make decisions at all, for decision-making is very wearing and poses considerable strain on the character. (Even a decision like raising the wages of janitors is wearing; for you may think you have decided to put up the wages of the janitors, when in fact what you have done in the eyes of a lot of people is to decide *not* to put up the wages of porters, night watchmen, stenographers, gardeners, and waitresses in the dining room.) Furthermore, there are often committees to whom responsibility can be passed. They exist, of course, to share responsibility, but it is tempting to give them no lead and just to "let things work themselves out." An administrator of science and scholarship can ride a long way on committees; but if he does, his institution will deteriorate for two reasons. One is that indecision is contagious: if the president wavers, the committees around him succumb to the futile phraseology so common among academics: "the time is not yet ripe;" or "this would set an awkward precedent," or that ultimate defensive inanity, "I am far from convinced," which means, "I don't understand this and I can't think of any arguments against it, but I'm going to oppose it." The second reason for positive guidance from the president is that, as a matter of experience, collective decision-making without leadership encourages a drift toward mediocrity.

"Unto everyone that hath shall be given" is a good recipe for excellence, but it is not common policy in faculty committees.

Second, *administrators must refrain from making decisions which other people ought to make.* In industry or in a government there is a hierarchy of decisions controlled from above. Decisions at the level of departments can be regarded as subdecisions arising from some broad general decisions arising from some general decision made at the top. Once the top decision is made, all subdecisions must be made accordingly. This is not true of decisions in universities. In a university department of chemistry, for instance, decisions about what shall be taught and what research shall be done have no reference whatever to most decisions made for the university as a whole. A president who issued directives to his professor of chemistry on research or curriculum would be regarded in Britain as in need of psychiatric treatment. Over such decisions as these (and they are in the long run the most important in the university) he has no authority and he must encourage the maximum diffusion of responsibility.

Third, *administrators must conceal their bright ideas.* Academic administrators encounter what Chester Barnard calls three "occasions of decision." They are called upon to solve problems referred to them by authorities outside the institution (such as an inquiry from the State as to how many students the university will be able to take in a given year); they are called upon to solve problems brought to them by departments under their administration (such as a request from the engineering department to put a penthouse on the roof); and they are expected to display initiative and a capacity for innovation. It is here that the academic administrator's technique has to differ from that of his opposite number in industry. In industry the very enterprise of the president creates confidence. In British universities naked enterprise on the part of a university president is regarded with suspicion, not to say alarm. If a British university president has a bright idea (and he does have bright ideas in his early years of office), it would be the height of ineptitude to publish it to his faculty, and fatal to issue a directive about it. He must unobtrusively—if possible anonymously—feed it into the organization at a low level, informally over lunch, and watch it percolate slowly upwards. With luck it will come on to his desk months later for approval, and he must greet it with the pleased surprise parents exhibit when their children show them what Santa Claus has brought them for Christmas. To do this over some reform urgently needed in the organization requires a singular degree of equanimity; but the university president who is not prepared to discipline his initiative in this way fails.

Fourth, *administrators must acknowledge divided loyalties.* The task of the administrator to promote the purpose of a university is complicated by the fact that his senior colleagues inevitably have to divide their loyalties between their profession and the institution they serve. It is not surprising that the first loyalty of a professor of chemistry should be to the profession of chemistry: to his fellow chemists working in the same field elsewhere, to the traditions of scientific integrity fostered by the Royal Society, to the professional standards of the Royal Institute of Chemistry. The basis for his self-esteem comes largely from outside the institution which hires and pays him; indeed even his esteem inside the institution depends largely on his reputation outside it. Of course, these loyalties may coincide very largely with those the professor has to the university; and for the most part there is no conflict. But it does mean that when some question concerning his own department is under discussion the professor does not naturally find it easy to examine the question as it bears on the university as a whole; he does naturally find it easy to see the question as it bears on the welfare of chemistry in the university. The university president has to make very large allowances for those areas of interest where loyalty to the profession and loyalty to the institution do not coincide. His skill is to balance the centrifugal forces of individuality which tend to pull the institution apart against centripetal forces—largely generated by himself—which tend to preserve the integrity of the institution.

Turning from the attitude of university presidents toward their faculties, my handbook would contain chapters on the attitude of the faculty toward the president. Very briefly, the university president should be regarded by the faculty as a delicate integrating machine into which you put information, and from which (if the information is properly coded) you get decisions. It is well to remember two things about this machine: The first is that you cannot expect him to make a decision unless you "programme" him properly. And the art of coding the information you feed into administrators is quite as difficult as the art of coding data for a digital computer. Some faculty members in Britain fail to appreciate this. Every university president has had the experience of being accosted by a professor who wants a new building, or an electron microscope, or a flock of research assistants at once—as though all the president needs to do were to get an order book out of a drawer in his desk and sign an order. The request comes with no supporting documents, or embeds it in thirty pages of irrelevancies typed in single space! It comes on to the president's desk (although the professor never thought of this) along with a dozen similar requests. The president has to transform this ill-prepared brief into a persuasive paragraph for his finance committee which meets in two days' time (and he may well have to do it at midnight after returning home from a Rotary Club dinner). If the professor fails to get what he wants, he will say the president has lost his punch; it does not occur to the professor that he himself may be at fault because he failed to code his request in an appropriate form.

The president-as-computer all the time integrates many diverse considerations into simple formulae which can easily be used for executive action for the benefit of the university. He may fail for any of three reasons: because he cannot elicit appropriate replies from experts (and this may be because the experts do not know how to "programme" questions to him); because having secured the information he cannot create a simple and persuasive decision out of it (because his own "integration mechanism" is at fault); or because his decisions underestimate the political component (they may be excellent in theory but not viable; they may overlook the adage that politics is the art of the possible).

I have commented on the president-as-computer. Finally, I turn to the president as a man, to ask one question: Is a career in science, such as Arthur Compton brought to the office of chancellor of Washington University, a good qualification for a university president? There are entries on both sides of the balance sheet. On the debit side there is the fact that the scientific mind is inclined to oversimplify. The strategy of scientific experiment is always to minimize the number of variables (that is, to hold the temperature or the pressure constant while the volume is changed). In administration there are always more variables than there are equations. The assumptions which are so invaluable in science—"this factor may be neglected" or "this condition was held constant"—must never be employed by the university president. No factor may be neglected. No condition is held constant. A second drawback of scientific training is the predisposition to suspend judgment. The need to suspend judgment occurs in administration, but to nothing like the same extent that it can and should occur in scientific research.

On the credit side of the balance sheet there are entries which are a great asset to the scientist who becomes a university president. One of these is the essential humility of the scientist. The scientific revolution destroyed the tyranny of dogmatic truth. For centuries Europe was bedeviled by the stifling effects of closed systems of knowledge which acted as hotbeds for bigotry and persecution and hatred. Since the scientific revolution, knowledge has become an open system. Truth is now tentative, not final and revealed. Error is now a rejected alternative to truth, not something evil and to be persecuted.

To have worked within this open system of knowledge is an immense advantage to any administrator, and for the academic administrator it is essential. Just as the senior scientist expects a fresh idea or a flash of originality from a young man in his laboratory—and is ready to welcome it even if it upsets his own cherished theory—so the university president must expect, and be ready to welcome, innovations from his faculty, even if they upset his tidy plans for the university.

Thus let us not underestimate the ethical value of science for the administrator. It cultivates humility, faith in one's fellow men irrespective of their age or status, a commitment to accuracy, a ruthless integrity over communication of thought, and a world view instead of a view limited by nationality or language or race.

business of the Royal Society is: To improve the knowledge of natural things . . . (not meddling with Divinity, Metaphysics, Morals, Politics, Grammar, Rhetorick, or Logicks)." One cannot consider the social function of science without meddling in some of these subjects. The risks of doing so were evident to Bernal himself, for in this same book he sternly criticizes the social sciences; but his conclusion is that the risks must be run. The present condition of mankind requires some scientists to get outside the framework of science and to influence the interactions of science with society.

In common with thousands of my generation I was driven to think about these matters after reading an earlier book by Bernal (1939), *The Social Function of Science,* published on the eve of World War II. The last two chapters of that book carried, in the idiom of twentieth-century science, the message of John Donne's *Devotions,* written three and a half centuries earlier: "No man is an Iland, intire of itself; every man is a peece of the Continent." It was not necessary to embrace Bernal's political views in order to be moved by his concern for mankind.

The Social Function of Science was an optimistic book. It deplored the public neglect of science and the starvation wages of finance for research. It warned that if society neglects science, science cannot serve society. But it was a book based on belief in the possibility of progress, and twenty-five years later when Bernal re-examined his thesis, he concluded that to a very large extent the book had fulfilled his original objective. He was still optimistic only more cautiously so. He wrote, in a passage which I take as my text: "If we can survive the dangers of the immediate present we have every chance of realizing a world so different from anything we have had before that the transition is greater than any which has occurred since the first appearance of humanity. . . . Between that world and the present, however, we clearly have to pass through a transitional period which will be one of great danger. . . . The operational problem remains of how to effect the transition with the minimum of strain and destruction" (1964). Today we are in the transitional period and there is no doubt about the great danger. It is constantly being analysed and diagnosed. But to bring some of the problems of this transition to the attention of scholars and scientists is not easy: first, it is difficult to gather reliable data on the subject;

second, the ideas cannot be communicated with close logic, based
on verifiable facts, to which the scientific community is accustomed.
It is the aim of science to propound conclusions which are independent of the attitude of the observer. In propounding conclusions
about society there can be no such aim, for the conclusions depend
on the attitude of the observer. All one can hope to do is to stimulate
reflexion; one cannot hope to establish definitive truth.

My theme starts from a paradox: the crisis of disillusionment
in western affluent societies was the successful landing of a man on
the moon. Until then large numbers of people were still prepared to
believe that the social benefits of science and technology were largely
fortuitous and the disorders of society were largely inevitable. But
at that point people realized that a wealthy nation could mobilize
enough skill and money deliberately to solve an incredibly difficult
technological problem. At the moment of triumph there was criticism, not of the achievement but of the goal. Many Americans,
writes Harvey Brooks (*New York Times,* January 12, 1970), regarded walking on the moon as "an arrogant piece of conspicuous
consumption." If this is what a sustained effort of planned technology can do, why is planning not successfully applied to other
goals: why not to the transport problem in cities, or to poverty, or
to the relief of the Third World? It is not convincing to say to the
man in the street (though I believe it is true) that these problems are
more difficult to solve than that of putting a man on the moon. People feel powerless to influence the goals to which the national effort
in science and technology is directed. Some of them resent this, and
their natural response is either to press for strict public control
guided by ethical imperatives, or to withdraw financial support: to
regulate what scientists do or to starve them.

Let me underwrite these assertions by a few examples. In the
United States, from 1945 to 1962, the allocation of federal funds for
research and development was increasing at the rate of about 20
percent per annum. In 1970 the total federal allocation for "R and
D" was only 2 percent more than the allocation for 1969—not
enough to cover the change in the value of money. This is a
symptom of a new attitude toward science on the part of the Congress. But it is not only the Congress which questions the scale of
investment in science. There is in the United States and to a less

extent in Britain, a widespread unease (amounting among some of the young to despair) because moral skills applied to social institutions have not kept pace with scientific skills applied to technological needs. Society, regarded as a nonlinear feedback system, is showing the signs of oscillation (hunting) which one expects when the homeostatic mechanisms, which should maintain an equilibrium between political decision-making and the state of technology, respond too slowly. Examples in Britain are the vacillations in our policies for dealing with higher education, urban transport, and the aircraft industry. These surges of uncertainty are exacerbated by the instant visibility of crises brought into our homes by television. We become hypersensitive to the contrasts between poverty and plenty, violence and the enforcement of law and order, the occasions of failure to choose socially desirable goals and the successful technology which achieves the goals which are chosen. There is an irony about all this. Over a generation ago the advanced western countries seriously upset the equilibrium of traditional communities in Africa by exporting technology to them; now the disequilibrium has spread to our own cities and affected our own communities. Observers as sober and responsible as Rabinowitch (1963) saw this coming: "The capacity of the democratic, representative systems of government to cope with the problems raised by the scientific revolution is in question."

One only has to look east to realize that political systems different from our own are not much more successful in adapting society to its contemporary environment (Price, 1965). It is significant that zealots of the New Left reject the communist pattern of politics as vehemently as they reject the capitalist pattern. They have no coherent alternative, but many of them have cultivated an ideology of antiscience. They question the very legitimacy of scientific thought. This is nothing new; indeed the opening chapter of Bernal's *Social Function of Science* recalls how Georges Sorel, over seventy years ago, repudiated the intellectuals of his time in favour of an emphasis on instinct and intuition: and Bernal warned his readers that this is the stuff of which Fascism is made.

Bernal's warning should not be ignored, nor should this recrudescence of antiscience in the 1970s be written off as the aberration of a few hippies. It has little in common with the antiscience of the nineteenth century which pestered Darwin and

Huxley. Its supporters are not drawn from the clergy, nor from simple people unfamiliar with science. Indeed some of its propagandists are scientists themselves, who complain that science, once frustrated by the rigours of poverty, is now frustrated by the demoralization of wealth. These people do not seriously suppose that the efficacy of scientific thinking for the understanding of natural phenomena is passing; we are not at a watershed similar to the one which divided Aristotle and the schoolmen from Galileo and Newton. But we are at a point when it is being seriously suggested that science ought to be practised under public scrutiny and restraint. In a book on science and society Rose and Rose (1970) ask, "How can control over scientific affairs be asserted?" and they go on to suggest that the committees which "allocate resources between disciplines and fields in the basic sciences must do so in the context of politically directed goals set by the community," and that the present "oligarchies" (presumably the authors mean the research councils) should be replaced by persons "openly elected by the scientific community from amongst its own number." The threat to society, writes another commentator, Roszak (1969), is "the paternalism of expertise within a socioeconomic system which is so organized that it is inextricably beholden to expertise." The innuendo is that if experts could be made irrelevant there would be no need to go through the tiresome process of becoming one. The counterculture offers a path to wisdom about nature which does not lie along the long dusty road of hard work. The more sophisticated prophets of antiscience, such as Ellul and Marcuse, are more reactionary than this. They encourage disaffiliation from the contemporary scientific culture on the ground that if its values are adopted, mankind will become enslaved by his technocracy. Indeed, they say, it is already happening. They too should not be dismissed as querulous eccentrics. For public enthusiasm for science, confidence in scientists, and undisputed willingness of nations to finance research, are very recent phenomena; and it is only about twenty-five years since they appeared; they could just as quickly disappear. So we should not leave unchallenged those who wish to impose politically directed goals on basic research, and those who embrace the counterculture of antiscience. They confuse, in my view, two quite different issues: the purposes for which science is done by scientists and the purposes for which science is used by society. Although this distinction is a trite one, it is necessary to restate it for the sake of my theme.

The achievements in basic research are possible only because the research worker is free from two constraints: he can disregard first causes; and he can disregard any purpose except that imposed by the inner logic of the discipline itself. He is therefore able to choose problems on two criteria only: that they are likely to be soluble and that the solutions will be relevant to current concepts in the discipline. The use of these criteria has one unfortunate side effect, namely that the intractable problems, because they are never tackled, come to be regarded as unimportant. (Thus classical problems in biology, such as the origin of a land flora, are neglected not because they have been solved but because they seem at present to be insoluble.) The framework of concepts in science owes coherence and strength to the fact that those who build it do not try to comprehend reality: they build from abstractions and simplifications. So it is evident to anyone who has done basic research that the problems to be tackled cannot be defined by persons outside the discipline, and that the solutions obtained are valid only within the framework of the discipline.

With mission-oriented science it is otherwise. The goal lies outside the discipline. The actual scientific work is still done by the methodology of basic science, but its intrinsic purpose is mediated by an extrinsic purpose. The influence of the extrinsic purpose may be weak, as in some kinds of medical and agricultural research which have a longrange generalized goal, such as a cure for cancer or the production of a drought-resistant wheat; or it may be strong, as in research to increase profits in industry or to devise defence against missiles. The old controversy, which has recently been sharpened by the Society for Social Responsibility in Science, is whether the scientist is competent to define the extrinsic purposes. It is another form of the question I raised earlier: is it part of the social function of science to determine goals?

The choice of extrinsic goals cannot be determined by the methodology of science. There are some who believe that if there were big enough computers and clever enough programmers and reliable enough data, then the social sciences could do for politics what the physical sciences have done for matter. I do not share this belief for two reasons. One essential input for political decisions is the prediction of public opinion toward the decisions, and the very process of seeking public opinion frequently changes it; MacKay (1963) points out that no complete description exists which would be equally valid whether or not the units were informed of it. Another essential input for political decisions is value judgment; this cannot be satisfactorily quantified. The social sciences can quantify the costs and benefits of this or that political choice; what they cannot do is to quantify, even through statistically analysed questionnaires, the value of the choice. It is on these grounds that I conclude that no mathematical refinement of the social sciences will enable rigid scientific methodology to be applied to the choice of goals for mission-oriented science. To this extent the antiscientists have a point. What they are reminding us—though they deplorably distort their own case—is that the scientific method can speak authoritatively about means in society, but it cannot be authoritative about ends. There is no straight path from fact to value. If we rely on science alone, questions of purpose will not be answered; and politics are about purpose.

The policy of government, that scientists should be "on tap but not on top," which was at one time briskly challenged by scientists, is now commonly admitted to be a correct policy by those who have a right to an opinion. Attachment to the methodology of science is, if anything, a disqualification for decision-making in politics; there was wisdom in the cynical remark attributed to William Buckley, that he would rather be governed by the first hundred persons whose names appear in the Boston telephone directory than by the Harvard faculty. The formula for success in science—simplification and abstraction—can be disastrous in politics. Nevertheless, the methodology of science does have a powerful contribution to make toward the choice of goals in mission-oriented research. It can introduce considerations which otherwise would not be taken into account. One familiar example is research into pesticides. The original primary goal in government-sponsored research was to control pests; and in industry-sponsored research to make profits. In the early stages it was nobody's business to examine "third party" interests, and it was not until persistent organochlorines had spread along the food chain and accumulated a thousandfold in the bodies of birds, that the goals of research were changed. The purpose of applied research in this field now is to produce nonpersistent pesticides. But how can these "third party" interests be safeguarded? A panel convened by the National Academy of Sciences has proposed that an independent body assess the consequences of new technologies and make public "third party" interests before the technology is introduced. I think one should not expect more than limited benefits from such a body, for it is notoriously difficult to predict the side effects of new discoveries. Bernal (1939, p. 198) gave a vivid example of this: the invention of aniline dyes, he wrote, brought starvation to a million Hindu agricultural labourers whose indigo was no longer needed. However much responsibility scientists take for the consequences of their work, is it reasonable that Perkin could have foreseen this effect of aniline dyes on Hindus? Or Einstein, in 1905, the translation of his equation into a bomb? Or Hertz, the employment of his discovery as a tool for dictators to control whole nations? Anything which smacks of research in the future is bound to generate scepticism and invite contradiction; a good example is the speculation about the possible effects on world climate of carbon dioxide from fossil fuels.

By the cautious use of modern statistical methods, very useful help can be given those who have to make choices in areas of uncertainty, and scientists, through their expertise in science, can influence these choices. But when it comes to making the extrinsic choice itself, the scientist steps outside the logic of his discipline and has to admit noncognitive elements into the equation. Like everyone else, he is expected to work within the political system which sustains him and to accept the fact that it is the politician, not the scientist, who is elected to represent the value judgments of the people.

There is another, and to my mind more effective, way in which scientists can influence the choice of goals. Let me try to explain how. The traditional functions of government are to maintain law and order, to defend the interests of citizens against foreigners, and to preserve the ethos of the nation. Our traditional political system is adapted to these functions. But modern governments have an additional function which has brought a new order of complexity into public affairs, namely to supervise and guide controlled technological and social change. It is hard to ascertain the will of the people over this new function, because the issues are believed to be too difficult for the people to understand, or for that matter for their representatives to understand. Too often parliaments seem to be no more than passive observers of such change. Thus, developments ranging from the making of Concorde to the use of nonbiodegradable plastics to wrap everything from razor blades to fish, seem to proceed with the faceless inevitability of the plot in Tolstoy's *War and Peace*. Such developments account for the naive pressure from the radical left to return to the participatory democracy of a New England village. There are many reasons for this sense of impotence. The reason relevant to my theme is that our system of higher education, which has been the formal apprenticeship for most of the technological goalsetters in Britain, gives no training in two essential areas: for politicians and administrators there is no training in how to use the inputs of science in the making of political decisions; for scientists there is no training in how to give due weight to noncognitive considerations in choosing extrinsic goals for science. When, for example, do the results of science justify political action? Should cigarettes be as illegal as pot? Should women in overcrowded countries be obliged to take the pill under risk of punishment, as some units of Australian soldiers were obliged, during the war in New Guinea, to take atebrin against malaria? Should airlines pay, through airport charges, for the noise pollution they cause and the proceeds be used to provide double glazing in all homes within ten miles of the runway? These are questions which cannot be answered within the framework of science alone or politics alone. Neither the scientist nor the politician can get from our system of higher education an expertise for dealing with such questions.

Upon this argument rests the case for a reappraisal of the function of science in universities and other institutions of higher education. But first there must be an understanding of the forces which shape these institutions.

A university, like an organism, is a product of heredity and environment. The heredity of the university is manifest as a consensus among academics about what a university stands for: excellence, objectivity, the cultivation of reason, the inherent value of knowledge—all the clichés emitted by vice-chancellors at graduation ceremonies. This consensus, if it is strong enough, generates a powerful inner logic which is inherited by new universities. The university environment is the social and political system which supports it. This acts through two main forces: the pressure of candidates to get in (customer demand) and the suction from employers drawing graduates out (manpower needs). The flow of public finance into universities depends on public satisfaction that due weight is given these two forces. So in all universities there is a dynamic equilibrium between the three forces of inner logic, pressure, and suction.

British universities are at present in a state of disequilibrium between these forces. The Robbins Report, a monumental exercise in logistics, propounded the doctrine that the size of our higher education system should be determined by the number of qualified candidates who seek admittance. The report wisely declined to base calculations on predictions of manpower demand. But less wisely it had practically nothing to say about what the goals of the system should be; it was assumed that the old inner logic would persist. All but a few of those now responsible for university policy are busying themselves with similar logistic problems. How should the predicted student population of 1980 be divided between universities and colleges in the public sector? Can the costs of mass higher education be trimmed by fuller use of buildings, a longer academic year, diluted staff/student ratios, student loans, residence at home? Those who speak for the universities have made their attitude clear. They dislike all the proposed measures to cut costs (even fuller use of buildings reduces flexibility and narrows the options open to students); and they defend the tenets of their conventional inner logic: no devaluation of the degree, no erosion of research, no more than a tentative sacrifice of depth for breadth—in a word, no radical reappraisal of goals.

Some critics denounce the policy of expansion by asserting that "more means worse." They have yet to make a convincing case; the evidence is inconsistent with their assertion. But already there is no doubt whatever that "more means different." If the consequence of expansion is not pursued, universities will find themselves giving higher education to about 14 percent of the age group in 1980 on the same assumptions as they held when they were giving it to about 4 percent of the age group in 1960. Students and the public will certainly question these assumptions; indeed they are doing so already.

Before I elaborate this point I must digress a moment to consider an important paradox about universities, to which Alvin Weinberg (1966), director of Oak Ridge Laboratory, has drawn attention. Universities are organized by disciplines. The unit is the department (this is true even in those modern universities which think they have discarded departments). Within the department the style of both teaching and research is discipline-oriented; it comprises the objective discussion and solution of selected problems *within* the discipline. Interdisciplinary studies are no more than protodisciplines. As Weinberg says: "In the university the specialist and analyst is king."

But the traditional function of universities is mission-oriented: it is to educate a selected cohort of people to serve society. Research is a function added only comparatively recently. Service to society calls for skill in resolving problems arising from social, technical, and psychological conflicts, and the equally difficult skill of living with the problems which cannot be resolved. "Since," writes Weinberg (1966), "these problems are not generated within any single intellectual discipline, their resolution is not to be found within a single discipline . . . In society the non-specialist and synthesizer is king."

The contrast goes deeper. Within disciplines the homeostatic mechanism, the adjustment of goals to circumstances within the discipline, is astonishingly efficient. Despite the volume of material published or reprinted, the more enterprising workers in a discipline soon get to know of important work being done in other laboratories, and they respond promptly to this feedback in their own research. The efficiency of adjustment within disciplines is to be found, too, in the curriculum. Lecture courses in science rarely fail to take account of recent research. By general agreement training for the professions in Britain is at a very high standard. Universities are successful in producing graduates who have a mastery of the methodology and techniques within a discipline and who are equipped to become scientific workers or scholars. But in an era of mass higher education this is not what most graduates become, and universities are certainly far less successful in matching their extrinsic goals to the circumstances of society. For its mission-oriented function the homeostatic mechanism of the university is quite inadequate.

The goals of British universities have changed before. There is mounting evidence that the time has come for new goals to be added to the old ones. In the past major reappraisals have been imposed from outside, by competition from other universities or under the influence of royal commissions led by men such as R. B. Haldane. Even the establishment of the Ph.D. in Britain owed much to diplomatic pressure upon the universities from Foreign Secretary A. J. Balfour for a device after the First World War to attract American research students to Britain (Ashby, 1963).

The indications are that the present need for a change in university goals cannot be met by minor adjustments in the present system nor by pouring more money into the present system and allowing it to grow bigger. What is needed is a thorough revision of the inner logic of universities before the forces of pressure and suction overbalance them. To influence this revision is likely to be a very important social function of science in the next decade, and perhaps the most effective way in which scientists in universities can exert their social responsibility.

The incongruence between the discipline-oriented training which most undergraduates receive, and the mission-oriented activities in which many of them wish to engage after graduation, is one of the causes of the present discontent in universities. In its shallow manifestations it takes the shape of demands for "relevance," by which the undergraduates may mean nothing more than instant recipes for solving social problems according to some preconceived political doctrine; but it is a justified discontent all the same, and if there is no response to it the antiscience counterculture will be reinforced. Obviously universities must continue to provide discipline-oriented training for all those who aspire to be specialists, and to be implacably opposed to any dilution of this training. For this reason if for no other, universities must remain centres of research. To segregate the best scientists in research institutes would be to cut them off from the best undergraduates; the line of succession would be severed. But the exponential phase of increase in basic scientific research is already over, and it would be nonsense to assume that the volume of research must inevitably increase in proportion with the increase in student numbers, just because staff/student ratios do not change. Some research may have to be rationed. Indeed the volume of research may already be above the final asymptotic level; it would be an interesting exercise to estimate how much pedestrian research is necessary in order to sustain the comparatively small volume of research of real significance.

Yet if the need for people to discover new science is diminishing, the need for people to combine science and common sense in the difficult art of technocratic decision-making is likely to increase. Mass higher education must not produce armies of research workers; it should produce people who can integrate scientific and political considerations at all levels, from nuclear defence to the siting of a sewage plant. The parameters for this sort of decision-making include scientific data (in a form which can be used for cautious prediction), estimates of practicability (it is no good making a decision which is stillborn), and a framework of principles (in the long run a nation holds in contempt those among its leaders whose decisions are based on mere expediency). One of the goals of universities should be to train people who can define the parameters and perform this sort of integration; these are the people who will determine the choices of extrinsic goals for the deployment of science and technology.

This is a recent problem to which universities have so far given only trivial attention. I say "recent" because universities have not, in the past, been places devoted exclusively to rational and objective thought. They were religious foundations in which ethos combined scholarship and faith; accordingly ends and means were indivisible. Our present anxiety is that unexceptionable ends within a scientific discipline can be combined with highly objectionable ends outside the discipline. Universities have rid themselves of the dogmatic constraints of the church and they reject indoctrination of moral principles; but this has left a vacuum into which the antiscience counterculture is seeping. The vacuum must be filled; scientists can fill it with something more profound and more socially useful than could the counter-culture.

But there are massive difficulties to this change, the chief of which is a stubborn inertia within the system itself. This is illustrated by the way some academics have reacted to one of the very few constructive responses to the logistic problems facing universities, namely the proposal made originally by Pippard (1968; Pippard,

Parkes, Nicol, and Deer, 1970) that undergraduates who enrol in faculties of science be given a two-year general education in science, regarded as "one of the arts and only peripherally as a technical skill" and terminating in a bachelor's degree; thereafter those who are competent and who wish to have professional training in science (perhaps a third of the total) should pursue intensive courses in their specialism for another two years. There are other interesting features of the proposal, notably an easy system of transfer from one university to another and between universities and polytechnics.

Pippard's proposal has two great merits. It could be achieved through a policy of accelerated evolution rather than through the hazardous alternative of revolution. And it has enough degrees of freedom to permit further and more fundamental changes; for (in my view) the proposal does not go far enough. If it is a social function of science to influence the determination of extrinsic goals for the deployment of science, the seeds for this expertise must be sown in universities. Within Pippard's proposal this could be done. At the end of the two-year bachelor course, students could elect to concentrate on discipline-oriented studies (as the proposal intends) or on mission-oriented studies. By the latter I mean not only the traditional ones, such as engineering and medicine, but studies in technocratic decision-making, not at all on the lines of present courses in public administration, but by means of case-history seminars on problems which require the integration of scientific, political, and ethical principles. The seminar run by Don Price at Harvard, on science and public policy, and some of the courses organized by F. R. Jevons in Manchester, are examples of what I have in mind. The aim of the seminars would be to take students through the dismaying experience of seeking principles, by which decisions requiring not only technology but also moral concepts can be solved. It is easy to think of topics for such seminars: the control of pollution in the Rhine (a most complex exercise in biology, law, economics and international relations); urban living and transport; industrialization in tropical Africa; the political implications of computers. I suggested earlier that the solution of such problems as these is harder than putting a man on the moon. People who participate in astronautics do so voluntarily, and there are comparatively few of them.

In the control of population, or traffic, or pollution, millions of people must participate, many of them probably unwillingly. These are problems in social engineering; they have a moral parameter, and since we no longer live in a society which prescribes rigid moral parameters, we must determine them empirically (that is what much of the propaganda against pollution is about). A poor substitute for faith some will say; but in a pluralistic society there is no better one.

What about the teaching staff for these seminars? Some of them would have to be imported parttime into the university. The men who took part in decision-making about the 300 GeV machine, the international conventions about oil discharges at sea, the siting of a third London airport, and the rejuvenation of the Thames, would have to be mobilized to help. Weinberg (1967) suggests that the pattern of the large mission-oriented laboratories, such as Oak Ridge, Los Alamos and Goddard, now be adapted for massive efforts to tackle the major social problems which disfigure existence and impair the quality of human life—race relations, the decay of cities, crime, and mass education. To exercise full educational effect, the laboratories should be closely linked to universities or polytechnics.

This is one way in which the overhaul of goals for universities must go beyond Pippard's proposals. There are other ways and the proposals are open-ended enough to permit this. If the two-year bachelor course is to be a success it must attract first-class scientists as teachers. This requires a change in the criteria for esteem in the scientific world. In the world of art there is an honourable place for interpreters. We honour Daniel Barenboim for interpreting Beethoven and Frank Leavis for interpreting Lawrence more than we would if they composed third-rate concertos or novels themselves. In science there is no comparable honour for the interpreter. If scientists do regard it as a social function of science to educate generalists into the humane use of science, the interpreters of science to generalists must be duly esteemed.

There is another contribution which scientists could make to this issue, namely to encourage rigorous research into the processes of higher education (Ashby, 1971). Much educational research has, unfortunately, a deserved reputation for being futile and derisory. I think this is because unimaginative workers apply numerate techniques (such as chi-square tests to evaluate the influence of television on learning ability) to irrelevant problems, and they do not question their premises (we are, for instance, embarking on mass higher education still encumbered by Plato's theory of education for an elite in a slave state.) When a man of distinction, such as Jean Piaget, applies his talents to this field, his work is very productive, and the Educational Testing Service at Princeton has published important work in this field. It would help if more scientists of acknowledged distinction would give thought to the educational questions which ought to be asked about the mass higher education to which this nation is now committed. As a first step every large science department might appoint one staff member to reflect in a sustained way about the goals of teaching the discipline of the department to those who will not become professionals, and to offer him recognition for doing so.

One of the objections to Pippard's proposal is that it would devalue the academic currency. This is incorrect; all the proposal would do is revalue one coin in the currency. Another objection is that the two-year B.A. would be a cheap product with a low market value and would cause frustration among those who leave the university without proceeding to graduate work. This is a reasonable objection which would have to be met. It could be met first by a change in the attitude of employers, especially those in local and central government; they would have to be persuaded to accept the two-year B.A. degree as the normal generalist qualification for administrative services and for parts of the teaching profession, on the understanding that at some later date it could be supplemented by further university study for which employees would be released on full pay. And second, there would have to be an "opportunity bank" to allow students a delay in taking up all or part of their grants for higher education, so that a student who left the university after two years could return five or ten years later to take some discipline- or mission-oriented course. Indeed, if a degree, like a passport, expired after ten years and was renewable only after reattendance at some place of higher education, we would have a built-in insurance against obsolescence. This would remove the disincentive to leave the university after only two years; and it would have a side effect of great importance for universities: it would help to ensure that everyone at a university wanted to be there. The new dynamic equilibrium be-

tween suction, pressure, and inner logic may be one in which universities, like museums and libraries, become places people attend any
time throughout life when they have a reason for attending, and
which they leave without dishonour or embarrassment when their
reason for attending is fulfilled. The sandwich-course concept could
last a lifetime.

To achieve this sort of equilibrium requires major change in
the attitude of society toward higher education. There is nothing
more frustrating than planning major change, partly because it is
impossible to be sure that a chain reaction of minor changes will end
in the desired major change, and partly because even simple changes
(such as the use of computers for keeping records) have side effects
(such as the IBM card revolution in Berkeley) which the planners
fail to foresee (though the side effects are occasionally foreseen by
novelists whose predictions, because they are in the form of fiction,
are disregarded by policy makers). Sometimes we cannot expect to
do more than "avert the thoughtless foreclosure of options." Nevertheless when we consider what will happen to universities—our prime
centres for basic science—if we simply extrapolate present trends,
then planning for change becomes indubitably a necessity. At present
we are not beyond extrapolating present trends. An official forecast
(Cloud, 1969) assumes an approximately exponential growth of
student numbers, increasing at the rate of about 5.3 percent per year
between 1971 and 1981, with an estimated total student population
of 835,000 (460,000 of them in universities) by 1981, at an annual
cost of about £980 millions. What is missing from this forecast is
any reflection on the consequences of doubling the size of the system
without reviewing social purpose. It has doubled before, nearly four
times since 1900, but each time the effects of doubling become more
complicated and the inner logic of the system comes under greater
strain.

One has only to reread Gibbon to be reminded that cultures
are not automatically equipped with devices for self-renewal. The
operational problem is, as Bernal wrote, how to effect the transition
to a humane technocracy with the minimum of strain and destruction. I reach a conclusion similar to his, for different reasons and from
a different political direction. I have used the university as an example
of a typical interface between science and society, to make the point

that although it is not a responsibility of the scientist himself to set extrinsic goals for the deployment of science, it is his duty to educate others to set these goals and to influence the way choices are made. These choices will determine the future not just of science but of western society. I am not one of those who believe that regimes must be upset and systems liquidated in order that the right choices be made. I do believe that scientists can profoundly influence choices through two activities: by making "critical and pluralistic attacks on the problems of society," and by creating a climate of opinion about the use of science in social policy among those who will be flooding into universities and colleges in the 1970s. These are activities which must be conducted not by heroic rhetoric but according to William Blake's prescription: in Minute Particulars.

Chapter IX

✿✿✿✿✿✿✿✿✿✿✿✿✿✿✿✿✿✿✿✿✿✿✿✿✿✿✿✿✿✿✿✿

A Community
of Scientists

*In the Middle Ages the Western world was united by a common
language—Latin—and a common religion. These cements of civilisation no longer hold the Western world together. But science and
technology act as a new cement, for they are accepted by people
irrespective of language, religion, or political doctrine. So science and
technology are a valuable force for cohesion among nations, and
implicit in them is a useful, if modest, code of morality. Thus, the
popularisation of science, as the basis for a common core of culture,
is a matter of the first importance for nations.*

121

In 1955 the conference of European Rectors and Vice-Chancellors met in Cambridge and an oration was given by Gilbert Murray, then in his ninetieth year. It was a memorable experience to hear a great European speak about the dangers threatening European civilisation. "You and I," he began, "are the survivors of a great catastrophe." Murray had seen the world of his youth crumble around him, but he was not in despair about the future. He held out some hope that the ancient moral prestige of Europe might be revived. The grounds for his hope lay not in science and technology, not in politics or diplomacy, not even in the intellectual life of Europe, but in a simple and ancient idea which he expressed in the words of Pliny the Elder: *Deus est mortali mortalem iuvare,* which I venture to paraphase, "Man's humanity to man—that is God."

Murray was a great European. Perhaps it is not inappropriate for his theme then to be elaborated now by an average European; for if European civilisation is to be preserved this will no longer be done by a handful of great men: it must be done by multitudes of average men, in ways which average men will understand. The impact of science and invention on the civilisation of Europe is a favourite topic for seminars, pamphlets, and learned sociological writings; indeed the subject lies most of the time hidden under heavy woolly clouds of words. I cannot hope to illuminate it; all I can hope to do is to select one proposition and to examine it with the eyes of an average European.

The proposition I select is as follows. Twice in history European civilisation has been one fabric. Twice in history the fabric has been torn. Science and invention have contributed to its destruction, but in science and invention lies one hope for its repair.

Let us reflect for a few moments on the traffic of ideas in Europe. Under the Roman Empire there was a constant coming and going across the roads of Europe of messengers, merchants, troops, and administrators. They carried with them the values and standards of Imperial Rome. This diffusion of ideas from one part of the Empire to another produced (as one historian has called it) "a singularly uniform and cosmopolitan civilisation throughout the Roman world, from which the local and provincial spirit was strikingly absent."

The barbarian invasions destroyed this early fabric of European society. The unity of ideas was replaced by numerous regional cultures. Europeans became provincial. Much of that provincialism survives to this day: witness the differences in local costumes, in the architecture of farmhouses, even in the traditions of haymaking in the valleys of Tyrol and Carinthia and Steiermark. Scattered through this patchwork of provincialism there appeared centres of culture—which constantly communicated with one another and which were united by the Catholic faith and the Latin tongue, a reticulum comprising monasteries, universities, cities, and courts— which held Europe together. Again along the roads of Europe culture was carried to the common people, this time through the gossip of pilgrims, the songs of jongleurs, the preaching (and often the political propaganda) of priests and friars, the talk of students, and the worldly wisdom of merchants who attended fairs and festivals.

The common language decayed; the common religion fragmented into sects; traffic between the centres of culture diminished. The barriers which severed Canterbury from Rome also severed Oxford from Paris. The channels of communication between university and university, city and city, became overgrown and stagnant. When the traffic of ideas again revived it was not a traffic between institutions or corporations; it was a traffic between individual scholars. The impulse which directed this traffic was no longer theology and the affairs of the Roman Church; it was the new philosophy and the phenomena of nature. The ideas of Galileo and Newton, Harvey and Descartes, Kepler and Boyle were cosmopolitan. Frontiers could not keep them out; sectarian zeal could not suppress them; differences in language could not conceal them. Boyle, for instance, read Galileo in Latin and Glaser in French, and regretted that he could not read the work of Germans except in translation; and although Boyle himself wrote in English his works were rapidly circulated on the continent in Latin editions.

In the seventeenth and eighteenth centuries science became one of the threads which held the fabric of European civilisation together. A traffic which began between individuals became consolidated in the interchange of publications between scientific societies and academics. Science became established in the universities during the nineteenth century and the universities began to regain a prestige in European life which they had lost since the Middle Ages. It is noteworthy that this prestige rested primarily on scholarship and not on education, on the university as a research institute and not on the university as a school for undergraduates. Gradually the universities became identified with science; great scientists worked inside rather than outside them. Today, notwithstanding the importance of such institutions as the Max Planck Gesellschaft in Germany and the Department of Scientific and Industrial Research in Britain, it is the universities which have once again become centres of high intellectual energy in Europe. They are continually in communication with one another, and the busiest channels of communication between them are in science. It is appropriate, therefore, that we should consider the balance sheet of science in Europe. What damage has science done, and what benefits has science brought, to European civilisation?

Science and invention are commonly charged with two crimes against contemporary Europe: every European lives in the shadow of a great fear, due to the invention of nuclear weapons; every European lives in a cheapened and decadent world, where standards of craftsmanship and taste have been destroyed by mass production and where values have been debased by mass communication. I do not believe that either of these charges should appear on the balance sheet of science in Europe.

It is indeed true that we live in fear of wholesale destruction and that war must be averted if Europe is to survive; but to live in fear is no new sensation for Europeans. We have always lived in fear. To be killed by an arrow or by plague is no less painful than to be killed by a bomb, and to starve is one of the worst ways to die. The mediaeval peasant walked in continual fear for his life and for the safety of his family. An arbitrary lord, a persecuting cleric, a ruined harvest, an infected rat, robbers, invading armies: any of these might at any time spell the collapse of his personal world. Living for him was as insecure as it is for a wild animal.

Let us not assume that we are the first generation to live in fear; we are not. There is, however, a great difference between the new fear and the old: the new fear is that death will extinguish not only ourselves and our families but our race and our whole civilisation; and that Europe will become a poisoned graveyard, to be cautiously colonised, as radiation diminishes, by socalled primitive peoples from remote parts of the world. This is fear of a different order, but it is a sophisticated difference. I think it may trouble your dreams and mine more than it troubles the dreams of the Paris taxidriver or the German miner or the British bus conductor, for they have more imminent anxieties than we have. Take Europe as a whole: fear is no new thing. What science has taken away with one hand she has given with another. It is more likely to be the sophisticated who suffer from a sense of doom.

The second charge against science and invention is that they have destroyed craftsmanship and cheapened taste, and that through mass production and mass communication Europe has become decadent and vulgar. Craftsmanship is certainly the affair of a smaller proportion of the population than heretofore and taste is shared by a larger proportion; the standards of the elite have certainly been smothered; but one has only to glance at the achievements of European science and technology to know that Europe is not decadent or (in the ordinary sense of the word) vulgar. Murray remarked on this in his oration: "In almost every form of physical competition we are constantly beating the record. In intellect we are making extraordinary advances; in social studies, care of public health, care of children and old people, treatment of criminals and the like we are making constant improvements."

Science and invention have not produced decadence, though they have changed standards, and (whatever the intellectuals of Europe may have lost) for the rank and file of Europeans these standards have practically all been improvements. The English labourer now has antibiotics for his wife at childbirth, free schooling for his children, airmail in three days from his son in Canada, leisure with television and football pools, and an inexpensive summer holiday trip to Ostend. This is improvement in its lowest terms. The English labourer can have also—if he wants them—the Hallé Orchestra and the Pasquier Trio and the Amadeus Quartet brought to his room, and the great literature of the world in Penguin Press for the price of a few cigarettes. It is only the sophisticated who share a sense of frustration. The cause of their frustration is not far to seek. In the nineteenth century, when people still believed in progress, social reformers and technologists were inspired by a programme to end slavery, to diminish child mortality, to prevent many diseases, to raise living standards, to establish universal free education; to eliminate drudgery from the factory, to create leisure in the home, to improve communications. Much of this has been achieved. Millions are happier because of these achievements. Only the sophisticated see the irony of it, for despite these achievements they find themselves no longer able to believe in progress.

These considerations lead me to make this point: that we should not measure the impact of science and invention on Europe by the sophisticated standards of university professors. For the common citizen of Europe science and invention have not increased the level of fear nor led to a decay in standards. When we come to draw up a balance sheet for science in Europe, fear and decadence should not be included on the debit side.

These two items are nevertheless examples of the ambivalent effects of science and invention on society. Medical science in underdeveloped countries reduces mortality only to generate famine. Even the humane triumphs of technology may be of dubious benefit to society. Are there similar examples of the ambivalent effects of science and invention in Europe?

There are. One example is the dubious benefit of improvements in communication. Napoleon's armies crossed the Alps no faster than the Roman legions did. Gladstone's voice carried no further than the voice of Pericles. But within a few decades of Napoleon's death the cities of Europe were linked by railways, and less than a century after his death an aeroplane had flown across the Atlantic. Within little more than a generation of Gladstone's death the voice of Winston Churchill was heard over the radio by millions of people, and less than a generation later the Prime Minister appeared on some five million television screens in Britain. London and Paris are not only within earshot; the journey from one to the other can be made in less time than the journey from Paris to Versailles took five generations ago.

Europe has contracted to the compass of a church parish. The instruments of communication are incredibly improved, but better communication has not led to closer communion. Europe has none of the cohesion of a church parish. Indeed our very proximity to one another only serves to emphasise our diversity. No Englishman is more stridently English than when he is traveling abroad; and it would be idle to pretend that understanding between the countries of Europe is any closer because they are now linked by air travel and radio and the tours of Thomas Cook. On the contrary, air travel has actually weakened some traditional bonds of understanding. The art of diplomacy, for example, rested in the old days on an ambassador and his staff who resided in a foreign country and who had some insight into the life of the people and the aspirations of the rulers of the host country. When these diplomatists negotiated on behalf of their country they were dealing with men they knew personally, in a cultural environment with which they were familiar. Diplomatists today still understand foreign countries and speak foreign languages, but their opportunities to negotiate are restricted. Whenever a critical piece of negotiation has to be done it is the Minister of Foreign Affairs who arrives by air to do it, in a city where he puts down no roots, among people whose temperament he has had no opportunity to study. And worst of all—for time is the lubricant for all diplomacy—the airborne Minister of Foreign Affairs cannot allow time for ideas to ripen or hints to mature; in a few hours he must fly back to his capital to prepare for another lightning journey to another country. It is little wonder that at the level of international politics countries misunderstand one another. The aeroplane has debased the art of diplomacy and in some ways it has vitiated the cohesion of Europe.

This is only one example of the ambivalent effects of technology on European civilisation. A similar story could be told about the effects of mass media. There is much on the credit side. I can sit in my home in Cambridge and listen to a concert from Düsseldorf or a political commentor from Geneva, or I can take a televised tour of the antiquities of Greece. Such richness was beyond the dreams of my grandparents. There is a debit side too. Newspaper, radio, and television could bring all that is best in European culture and all that is significant in international affairs into the homes of millions of Europeans; but this is not what happens—not in Britain at any rate. The newspaper which most Londoners read gives more prominence to a sex crime in Kensington than to the European Common Market. The radio services—those within the provinces of the United Kingdom—are not sensational, but they do emphasise local and parochial activities: Scottish music or Ulster folklore or Welsh poetry. Through the popular organs of mass communication the common man is not sufficiently stimulated to look beyond the horizon of his own region. He is constantly reminded that he belongs to London or Scotland: he is rarely reminded that he belongs to Europe. When national emotions are aroused these instruments for mass communication become weapons for progaganda, exciting hostility and exacerbating national differences. In the hands of dictators they become the most disruptive force in Europe, for they take captive the minds of men and they make possible a terrifying concentration of power. As Aldous Huxley (1947) wrote: "never have so many been manipulated so much by so few." We have to conclude that the technologies of communication must be entered on both sides of the balance sheet for science and technology in Europe.

Let us now turn to the credit side of the balance sheet. The clear and undisputed benefit which science confers on Europe, and indeed on the whole literate world, is that it deals in universals. By this I mean that the theories held about natural phenomena are independent of latitude and longitude, of race colour, and religion, of language and politics. There is a common faith in Boyle's Law and Ohm's Law, whether the believer lives in Moscow or Rome, Paris or Peking. And so when two Europeans talk about science the differences between them become irrelevant. One may be a communist of Magyar blood, the other may be a Nordic capitalist; one may be a devout Catholic, the other an unbeliever. When they talk about science they are united by thousands of assumptions which they share in common and by a vast mass of propositions to which they both subscribe. They are united not only by common beliefs in the particular science in which they are both experts, but by a willingness to accept on trust the common beliefs of other scientists in fields outside their own expertise. They share a common faith in science which is as stabilising intellectually (though not in other ways) as the common religion shared by their ancestors five centuries ago. This common faith is not cemented by authority but by consensus. Wherever science is pursued in Europe there you find a centre of cosmopolitanism. The differences between men of different nationalities are minimised, their common understanding of the world of nature is manifested. Science is undoubtedly a force of cohesion among the scientists of Europe.

The scientists of Europe are obliged to submit to this force of cohesion which binds them to other countries. They must constantly study and take account of scientific work elsewhere, even if it is done by citizens of a country with which they have nothing else in common. A Roman Catholic chemist from Italy cannot disregard the work of a Presbyterian chemist from Scotland, on the grounds that the Scots chemist speaks a different language and worships in a different church. One has only to glance at the bibliographies at the end of research papers to realise the interdependence of the scientific world. Every laboratory in Europe is constantly changing scientific strategy and modifying research programmes in the light of work done in other laboratories. The scientists of Europe are united not only by a common faith but by obligations to a common faith. Provided a piece of research fulfils the unwritten rules of evidence for scientific discovery, it is accepted and incorporated in the fabric of science.

Faith in science is faith on a narrow front. One can predict the ethics of a man sincerely dedicated to the Sermon on the Mount or to the *Encheiridion;* one cannot predict the ethics of a man sincerely dedicated to Newton's laws of motion. Nevertheless let us not underestimate the ethical value of science in international affairs. The scientific revolution has produced a "formula for tolerating error." This is at least a modest step forward. It has led already to a widespread recognition that both truth and error can be challenged, and when they are each must submit itself to examination.

If there is to be cohesion in Europe, nothing is more necessary than a formula for tolerating error. All of us have a childlike propensity for believing we are right. Englishmen believe it right that they should continue to use their preposterous weights and measures and to drive on the left-hand side of the road, and Finns believe it right to go on speaking Finnish despite the fact that most foreigners find it too difficult to learn. Over such divergences as these we have learnt tolerance. We still must learn tolerance over larger issues and it is here that the scientist's attitude to knowledge is relevant. If scientific knowledge is an open system, surely political knowledge should be an open system too.

On the credit side of the balance sheet for science in Europe we can put, first, a new interdependence which unites the scientific laboratories of Europe as closely as were the cathedrals and priories and abbeys of mediaeval Europe. Second, we can put a common faith in science which is shared by thousands of Europeans and which could become a foundation from which to explore and understand their differences. Third, the scientific revolution has destroyed the tyranny of dogmatic truth—truth as our ancestors understood it—and has put in its place a formula for tolerating error in others.

It is no exaggeration, therefore, to say that the scientists and scholars of Europe comprise a coherent group, preserving their national differences but sharing common beliefs and common aspirations. Universities, since they are the chief centres of scholarship in Europe, are united by science into one pan-European community. This is a precious asset in the balance sheet for science in Europe.

There is no cause to be complacent about this asset; it is presently ineffective because it is in the hands of too few people. The hope for Europe depends upon cohesion among whole populations of Europeans, not solely among a handful of intellectuals. One of the paradoxes of modern universal education is that the common man today is less in touch with what is best and most significant in European civilisation than his ancestors were five centuries ago. The civilisation of the Middle Ages filtered down to the common man through religion. The common man lived in wretched conditions: he was condemned to the state of life into which he had been born; his liberties were restricted. Nevertheless he received through his church some share of the culture of Europe. The disputations of the schoolmen coloured the sermons from his priest; week by week he heard Palestrina's music; as he knelt at Mass his eyes rested on an altarpiece by Van Eyck. The Universal Church was the source of education as well as religion; through its influence the remotest villages of Europe were irrigated from the central rivers of learning. In making this contrast between the Middle Ages and our own day I do not mean to infer that there is no popular culture in contemporary Europe—far from it—but contemporary popular culture exists separately from what the English call highbrow culture. Undoubtedly some cohesion is conferred on millions of Europeans through their common interest in Hollywood movies, rock music, and boxing; but it is not the sort of cohesion which withstands nationalism and racial prejudice as does the tradition of science and scholarship. If the assets of science are to benefit the balance sheet of science in Europe, the common man must be brought to understand something of the objectivity, the humility, the tentativeness which characterise a scientist when he is thinking about science. The common man must be brought to understand that—whatever else may divide Europe—European science is indivisible. This understanding, notwithstanding all the popularisation of science by television and radio and press, we have so far failed to propagate beyond a narrow circle of well-educated citizens.

The interpretation of science to the common man is essential if science is to contribute to the cohesion of Europe, and I venture to suggest that, in Britain at any rate, a good deal of the interpretation of science is of the wrong kind for this purpose. So often we do not patiently explain how scientists work, but rather we exhibit, like showmen, the mysteries and marvels of invention and discovery. The marvels of science have good entertainment value and there is no reason why people should not be entertained by science, but this does not contribute to the cohesion of Europe.

The immense prestige of science, especially among those who do not understand what science is about, carries a potential danger. The danger is that the scientist may come to be regarded as an initiate in some esoteric cult, a withdrawn and distant priesthood, whose influence on the common people of Europe arises from a superstitious regard for his powers and not upon an understanding of his work. This danger is more likely to appear in Europe than America or Russia, for in European countries we still reserve higher education for a comparatively small proportion of the population. The vast majority of Europeans still depend on radio, television, and the popular press for their understanding of science. These organs of mass communication inevitably appeal to the emotions rather than to the intellect; they evoke wonder, surprise, and fear rather than understanding. Anyone who has tried to use mass media to interpret science to the layman knows how much more difficult it is to teach than to entertain, and how dangerously easy it is for the scientist to become sacerdotal about his subject. Who has ever heard of a television programme erplaining how often research *fails* to make discoveries. It is important to avert a danger inherent in the very prestige of modern science. To fail to do so would be to put an entry in the debit side of the balance sheet.

If science is to contribute more to the cohesion of Europe the values of science must be interpreted to the common man. This is an educational problem of great difficulty. Dock workers, miners, bus-drivers, textile operatives, are not interested in the methodology of science. How can such men be persuaded that modern science and technology have made them indivisible from their fellow Europeans? I have no solution to this problem; only two suggestions which perhaps might provide foci for discussion.

One is a small practical suggestion about the popularisation of science. Every experimental scientist recognises that craftsmanship is important in research. Discovery owes much to the technician. For example, the history of cytology in the nineteenth century is largely the history of microscopes. As soon as craftsmen were able to grind better lenses, biologists were able to learn more about cell structure. In the popularisation of science much more could be made of the essential part played by technicians, craftsmen, and instrument-makers. Here is a link between science and the nonscientist. Through emphasis on the element of craftsmanship in science it may be possible to enlist the interest of the man who works with his hands, and to make him feel that he is not just a spectator, but an essential actor, in the modern scientific age.

The second suggestion is that universities assume a greater responsibility than they have for interpreting science to the common man and that they study intensively how to do it. This is an activity which the Russians have tackled more vigorously than we have in the West. The Academy of Sciences of the U.S.S.R. has an institute for the interpretation of science to the public. Some of the techniques used by this institute are very effective. It is astonishing to hear a chauffeur or a postman discussing cosmic rays at a level you would not find among similar folk in England or Germany. It would be very encouraging if the universities, which quite properly regard themselves as carrying some responsibility for the cultural cohesion of Europe, were to take steps to ensure that the man in the street understand and feel he shares three things about modern science: that it is cosmopolitan; that it is undogmatic; that the obligatory cohesion which already exists among European scientists and scholars is a nucleus around which political and economic cohesion might grow. This is an age when the universities have a unique opportunity to influence the history of Europe. Since the fourteenth century they have not enjoyed such prestige nor played such a part in the affairs of state. For generations history flowed past them and they made scarcely a ripple on the surface. Today the decisions of governments are embarrassingly dependent on scientists and technologists, many of whom are based in universities.

Scholars and scientists and technologists are seeds round which international goodwill might crystallise; but neither they nor the universities where they work can alone suffice to restore the fabric of Europe. If that is to be done, goodwill and tolerance must become endemic among millions of average Europeans. Science can help to spread goodwill and tolerance but faith in science alone will not solve Europe's problems: all it can do is to reinforce an older and deeper faith, the faith of men in mankind. We are brought back to the words of Pliny the Elder guoted by Gilbert Murray: *Deus est mortali mortalem iuvare.*

Chapter X

❁❁❁❁❁❁❁❁❁❁❁❁❁❁❁❁❁❁❁❁❁❁❁❁❁❁❁❁❁

Mass Higher Education

Three major environmental forces are pushing higher education towards vocationalism while the internal heredity of universities retains its non-vocational aim. Mass systems of higher education can offer excellence in both vocational and non-vocational programs if universities do not permit their non-vocational programs to be used by employers as screening devices for jobs, if they maintain opportunities for intellectual talent and avoid the inappropriate use of cost-benefit analysis, and if they develop mission-oriented studies as well as discipline-oriented programs.

Before one considers the implications of mass higher education, a semantic distinction is necessary. This distinction is best introduced by an analogy: everyone ought to have as much food as he needs, but not everyone needs or wants to be fed on caviare. Or, everyone in a society which can afford mass education is entitled to as much education (primary, secondary, postsecondary) as he needs, but not everyone needs or wants what we in Britian call higher—as contrasted with further—education.

Another semantic distinction concerns the term "higher education," which generally includes all postsecondary education, but which in Britain is restricted to mean university study. So I have to distinguish between vocational higher education and nonvocational higher education. Notice that this distinction cuts across some familiar boundaries. It puts into the same category the education provided by the faculty of medicine at Cambridge and by the department of catering at Colchester Technical College; and it puts into the same category Oxford Greats and Workers' Educational Association courses on archaeology. The boundaries between vocational and nonvocational higher education are blurred, but by and large vocational higher education qualifies a person to pursue a specific vocation or profession; nonvocational higher education does not. It may seem a perverse distinction, but I hope to show that it does make sense.

Higher education, defined in this way, is certain to become more than a minority interest. It has already, in two generations, increased by an order of magnitude, and it will do so again before the end of this century. That is why several countries have carried out sophisticated exercises such as the Robbins report in Great Britain (*Higher Education,* 1963), the reports of the Council for Higher Education in Germany (Wissenschaftsrat, 1960), and the colossal encyclopedia, already in some thirty volumes, of the Carnegie Commission on Higher Education in the United States. Yet in all these thousands of pages there is something missing. They go into great detail about increase in size of the system, about how the enlarged system shall be financed, about the way to make the system accessible to all who need to enter it, about the cost effectiveness and efficiency of the system. But they have comparatively little to say about whether the system should change and the function it should fulfill in the society of tomorrow.

To me it is clear that the system will have to change in all countries which undertake mass higher education. "More" does not mean "worse," but undoubtedly "more means different." Already our plans for expansion may fail to meet the needs of the majority for whom the expansion is planned. What are the educational implications of "more means different" in mass higher education?

Let me offer a conceptual framework into which facts and arguments can be conveniently fitted. It is characteristic of higher education systems that they are strongly influenced by tradition. They display what a biologist calls phylogenetic inertia. This is not surprising, for one of their functions is to conserve and transmit the cultural inheritance. It is characteristic of them, too, that from time to time they adjust themselves—sometimes painfully—to the social environment which surrounds them. There is an analogy, therefore, between these systems and biological systems: they are the resultant of hereditary and environmental forces, of nature and nurture. So universities, for instance, have everywhere a generic similarity, and yet they differ greatly from one nation to another.

There are, therefore, internal and external forces acting on higher education systems and when all is well there is an unstable equilibrium between these forces. At present there is a worldwide instability in higher education systems, and these systems are shifting, one hopes toward fresh equilibria which will be different for different societies. But while the movement is going on there are strains and anxieties; none of us know where the new equilibrium will lie. That is why it is disappointing that so much emphasis, by governments, by the press, and indeed within the systems themselves, is on how to expand, how to pay for expansion, and not on how to change.

There are three main environmental forces acting on systems of higher education. One is *customer demand*: the pressure of students to get into colleges and universities and to pursue the curricula they want when they get in. A second force is *manpower needs*: the "suction" drawing graduates into employment, and therefore influencing curricula and certification. The third force is the *patron's influence:* higher education systems are not (they never have been) supported by customers or employers; they are nowadays under the patronage, that is, the ultimate financial control, of the state.

When forces in the social environment press for change in a higher education system they are likely to encounter two kinds of hereditary resistance. One is the inertia of the system to any change; and this is a virtue (though often an infuriating one), for systems do need some stability and the influence can be capricious. The other resistance is not a negative one and it is much more important; it is the belief in the purpose of the system which is held by those who are engaged in it. A higher education system has its articles of faith by which its practioners live, and these are not always consistent with the demands which society makes on the system. These hereditary forces constitute what I call the "inner logic" of the system. It may show itself as the determination of a technological university to foster sandwich courses, or the determination of a faculty of arts to resist noncognitive material in its curriculum, or the determination of a physics department to refuse a research contract. The inner logic does for higher education systems what genes do for biological systems: it preserves identity; it is a built-in gyroscope.

The balance between these forces differs in different countries. In the Soviet Union manpower needs and the patron's influence play a predominant part, and inner logic is muted. But in the Academy of Sciences, to which the more distinguished scholars belong, inner logic plays a great part. In the United States customer demand has had a predominant influence, both on the size of the system and on its astonishing diversity; but the graduate schools are guided by inner logic. In Germany, and until recently in Britain, inner logic has played a predominant part in the universities, but in Britain the influence of the social environment (customer demand and manpower needs) has operated most noticeably on colleges in the public sector; in Germany on the schools of technology. In all these systems—even in the Soviet Union—there have been healthy checks and balances between the forces. When there are no healthy checks and balances (as, for instance in some of the universities of India and Latin America, where the influence of inner logic is very weak)' the systems fail to serve their societies well.

We are at a moment of history when the balance of forces in systems of higher education all over the world is upset by social changes, and fascinating realignments of forces are taking place. The central motive of Robbins was to give priority in education to customer demand; a place in fulltime higher education for every qualified candidate. This is already diminishing the influence of inner logic, and at the same time the influence of the patron—the State—is increasing. There is a backlash in the United States against the unmotivated student: the customers (estimated at 30 percent) who really do not want to be there; and a backlash too against one manifestation of inner logic: the determined efforts of many universities to devise freshman and sophomore years of general education. In Germany the supremacy of inner logic, cherished by the professoriate, has been shattered by the recent legislation for university governance, which prescribes that membership of all the main university committees should include one third professors, one third junior staff, and one third students—the so-called *Drittelparität*. The shifts in equilibrium are complex and very diverse; many of them seem to be strengthening the influence of the social environment at the expense of the cultural heredity of the systems.

Forces from the social environment are capricious. It is therefore essential that those engaged in higher education should decide what each sector in the system stands for, that is, their inner logic; and (in this context I am in favor of the "university militant") defend it against erosion from the currents of society. But the dilemma is that there is no consensus, even within one sector of the system in one country, about what higher education systems do stand for. In Britain, for instance, should polytechnics offer a liberal education; should they promote research? Should universities offer a choice of easy and hard bachelor degrees? We are assuming (on both sides of the Atlantic) that growth, diversification of curriculum (such as area studies and interdisciplinary mixes), and changes in mode of government (such as student participation) will solve our problems. They will not. Our problems centre round a definition, for each sector of higher education, of its inner logic; which is another way of putting my question: what are the implications, for the inner logic of educational systems, of "more means different"?

Higher education systems offer both vocational and nonvocational curricula. A common controversy is whether these two kinds of curricula should be in one kind of institution (the multiversity) or in separate, different kinds. I think this controversy is fruitless and futile. Whether higher education is organised in a binary or unitary system is merely a matter of logistics; the boundaries of our binary system are dissolving before our eyes, and a good thing too. Universities have always mixed vocational and nonvocational studies, and polytechnics are already doing the same. It is important to reflect on the changes which may be necessary in these two kinds of education, wherever they occur in the higher education system.

Vocational higher education ends in certification of recruits as fit to enter vocations and professions. In many fields this education is obsolete in a decade or so, but the certification remains valid. It is a serious indictment of the higher education system in Britain (and indeed of most of those elsewhere) that there is no provision except at Birkbeck College and in the Open University for the easy readmission of adult students for *extended* postexperience courses, to accord with the pace of technological and social change. But if higher education systems are to take on this burden, there will need to be a corresponding economy in the vocational courses given to young students. The Carnegie Commission has already proposed ways to do this for medical education, by cutting a four-year course to three years and offering honourable exits to higher education at two-year intervals; and Brian Pippard has proposed ways to do it in Britain for the education of scientists, by restricting professional training to those who will become professionals. As more and more people aspire to postsecondary vocational education, the reasonable response would seem to be to offer it in modules in such a way that engineers, doctors, accountants, even lawyers, renew their certification by returning to take modules in their expertise every decade or so throughout their careers. There is at present a built-in discrimination against the adult student. One realises how powerful it is when one immediately thinks of eighteen to twenty-one year olds at the mention of "the undergraduate age group," or "people of college age," or "the student culture." At the mention of the "museum" or "library" age group, the impression is not the same. This discrimination must be dispelled if we are to have successful mass higher education.

It is right and proper that employers, professional associations, and the state should influence vocational higher education; but the authority for nonvocational higher education must be inherent in the inner logic of the system itself. This means that those of us who are engaged in nonvocational higher education must reach some consensus about why we are engaged in it. There is no problem in justifying to the public why they should pay for mass higher education for vocations and professions. But a great deal of mass higher education is going to be nonvocational, whether in universities or polytechnics or other further education colleges. Why should the public pay for mass nonvocational education?

The difficulty is that nonvocational education is pursued for a variety of motives. One motive which must be resisted is the pursuit of nonvocational higher education solely in order to get certification for a job. The employers must be reformed first in this regard. They are doing a great disservice to higher education by using degrees and diplomas, which are quite irrelevant for the jobs they are filling, as filters for selecting candidates. As more and more young people go to college, employers raise the educational standards they require, yet the educational credentials essential for getting a job often have little to do with how well an individual performs that job. I suggest that if nonvocational higher education is to serve its real purpose (which is to civilise people) it ought not to attract people who only want to be certified, not civilised. I can see only one way in which higher education systems can promote this, and it would be an unpopular way: *not* to certify nonvocational education, but simply to do what was common in Scottish universities in the nineteenth century—issue class certificates to those who have attended courses and done the required written work.

In universities particularly we have, I believe, been diverted from the true goal of education (only in some subjects) to the false goal of certification. Perhaps one of the uncovenanted benefits of mass higher education will be that a certificate which almost everyone possesses will no longer be coveted by anyone. We can in any case expect that as a greater proportion of the age group acquires certificates of higher education, the salary differential between certified and uncertified will diminish. But, in my view, we who are engaged in higher education should do all we can to hasten this process. The way to get rid of elitism is not to lower standards but to offer a wide range of standards (which the whole system but not the university sector is trying to do), and to do nothing which accentuates the status gap between those with different education (the gap is maintained, for instance, by degrees, gowns, classification —or at any rate the publication—of examination results). Our responsibility is to rid ourselves of the idea that an educated person is socially superior.

My claim that the purpose of nonvocational education is to civilise people is an example of a motive for higher education which must be encouraged. It is a caricature with that core of truth which caricature contains that vocational education is concerned primarily with means and nonvocational education with ends. The primary aspiration which a good teacher has when he is teaching any non-vocational subject in higher education (history or German or physics, for example, to students who are not going to become historians or linguists or physicists) is to carry the student from the uncritical acceptance of orthodoxy to creative dissent over the values and standards of society. Polanyi (1962) puts this clearly: the professional standard of science (and it could be said of all knowledge at the level of higher education) must "impose a framework and at the same time encourage rebellion against it." The beneficial effect of nonvocational higher education is to lift the student from a level of conventional moral reasoning, to what Keniston (1972) describes as the postconventional level, where students are deliberately challenged "to reexamine assumptions, convictions, and world views they previously took for granted." In pluralistic society it is essential that as many people as possible are lifted from the conventional to the postconventional level. I can do better to illustrate this argument than to paraphrase two arguments made by Keniston: It is well known that the half-life of some technologies is less than the life span of an ordinary man or woman. We now realise that one consequence of this is that the half-life of some social institutions and cultural and moral values is just as brief. People may not only become uneducated for the job: they may become uneducated for living. Therefore individuals have to reorient themselves during their lifetimes to new cultural and moral values as well as to new technologies: "If . . . technologies, definitions of truth, and conceptions of morality change within the individual's lifetime, ironclad adherence to one set of skills, to one view of the truth, or to the present moral standards of one subculture will leave the individual stranded, isolated, and displaced before he reaches middle age" (Keniston, 1972).

We see the menace of obsolete, even atavistic, value judgements all around us. The prime aspiration in nonvocational higher education is to keep our society pluralistic, humane, tolerant, open to alternative truths, and able to distinguish prejudice from error.

Most of nonvocational higher education falls short of this aspiration. But there is evidence that enlightenment has changed for the better the values of the "common man." We no longer tolerate slavery, child labour, or the worst forms of pollution. It is likely that education has greatly contributed to these value changes. This is the justification for asking the public to support nonvocational higher education on a mass scale. "Seen in this light," writes Keniston (1972), "the question is not whether we can afford universal higher education, but whether we can afford to be without it."

Many controversial implications arise from this theme. One is that mass higher education, like mass production, is a different thing from "handmade" education or production. A lot of it is impersonal, even using techniques of videotape, TV, and correspondence courses. The experience of the London external degree and the promise of the Open University show that this can be done successfully. But there are still two kinds of education which demand a personal teacher-student relationship, for which there is no substitute. One is vocational, the education of master craftsmen and artists. To become an engraver on glass, or a silversmith, or a solo violinist, there is only one recipe: to be apprenticed to a master and to submit to his regime of discipline. The other is nonvocational, the education of the innovators in intellectual life and the pacesetters in cultural and moral standards. For this, too, there is only one recipe: the sustained dialectic with a master whose own intellectual and cultural achievements are distinguished. So, within the system of mass higher education, there must be opportunities for the intellect to be stretched to its capacity (the critical faculty sharpened to the point where it can change ideas), by close contact with men who are intellectual masters. Not many students are fit for this austere discipline or are willing to submit to it but those who are must be able to find it, or the thin clear stream of excellence on which society depends for innovation and for statesmanship will dry up. Personally I am not in favour of herding such talented students into special institutions. Talent and mediocrity can share the same central heating plant and cafeteria, and they should, for talent has to learn to operate in a world of mediocrity. Talented people should not be considered socially superior.

A second provocative implication arises from the first one. Cost-benefit analysis can be applied to vocational education; a vocational qualification probably puts up the earnings of the person who possesses it and possibly benefits the economy. But cost-benefit analysis applied to nonvocational education is nonsense; indeed such education may be counterproductive, producing men and women who not only eschew high-income careers for themselves but even reject and oppose the commonly accepted norms of Western society, such as the necessity for an ever-increasing Gross National Product. Cost-benefit analysis can doubtless suggest ways in which mass higher education can be more efficiently conducted; but it would be positively inefficient to try to increase the efficiency of that sector devoted to minority "handmade" education. We still cannot teach or learn at this level any faster than did our ancestors in medieval Oxford. An illuminating comment I heard recently in a discussion of the arts is equally applicable to this level of higher education: despite all our advances in technology it still takes three manhours to play a forty-five-minute quartet. Technology enables more people to hear the quartet; but technology never will improve the productivity of the performers.

Finally there is another and different conceptual framework which is helpful in some discussions of higher education. A person's capacity to contribute to society can be broken down into three different kinds of skill: skill in working with ideas, skill in working with things, skill in working with people. Traditionally in Britain the first skill and the third are learnt if at all "on the job." Everyone needs a mixture of all three skills, though in different proportions. What we are now experiencing is pressure from the young to put more emphasis in higher education on the skill of working with people. I believe the young are right. And if they are, mass higher education must take account of this.

How is this to be done? Not by discussing noncognitive, affective approaches to experience. These approaches are an essential ingredient of living, and institutions of higher education should provide opportunities for them as they do for physical recreation and for catering. But they should be part of the social environment of a college, not its narrow social purpose; that (I believe) ought to be confined to the cognitive, rational approach to experience, simply because that is what the teachers are competent to teach.

Middle East oil embargo) provokes feedback from society to its institutions (especially to legislatures); the institutions respond to restore the equilibrium. At the institutional level, disturbance similarly stimulates response.

We know already that the vulnerability of technological societies and their institutions is not due to lack of feedback (indeed the mass media saturate institutions with feedback, much of it distorted and untrustworthy). Their vulnerability is due rather to the incapacity of institutions to sort out which feedback messages are significant and to respond to them effectively and swiftly. Meadows (1973) writes that a "mismatch exists between the time span of development of environmental problems and the time horizons of institutions designed to deal with these problems." I am highly critical of Meadows' computer simulations and the doom which they forebode, but some of his comments, especially this one, are perceptive. It is natural (and this is the point which Meadows is making) that legislatures should select and respond to short-term issues, for stands on these issues win votes at the next election. Changes whose full effects may not be felt for a generation are bound to have a lower political priority. And yet the response to these changes will determine the destiny of industrial societies.

Legislatures are only one of many institutions in society. Universities are another, and they, too, have to sort out the feedback messages they receive and respond to them. No one can charge universities with not trying to respond. At no time in their history have they been so introspective, so eager to serve society, so ready to admit the need to change. But somehow this earnestness does not add up to any consensus about how to change—in what direction, toward what goals, by what procedures. Universities have become multipurpose institutions, and there has been an accretion of functions over seven centuries. To the function of seminary for the learned professions has been added finishing school for gentlemen, research institute, community service station, and (in the minds of a vociferous minority) nursery for social revolution. All universities now undertake more than one of these functions and some try to undertake the lot. The problem of adaptation of universities amounts to this, that each of these functions involves a different response of the university to society.

Let us look at this problem by considering the challenge to the university as seminary, as research institute, and as finishing school. As a seminary for the professions, the university is concerned with the balance between supply of and demand for graduates. This function implies a sensitivity to manpower demands. A recent example is the fall in the market for Ph.D.s in science and technology on both sides of the Atlantic. In 1959 the conference of European Rectors and Vice Chancellors chose as one of its themes the shortage of Ph.D.s. Today similar conferences have chosen as a theme the superfluity of Ph.D.s. Here is a clear illustration of mismatch between an institution and the society it serves: the response of the institution has been too sluggish. But the problem is much more complicated than this. The university is also a research institute, and for this purpose it needs to have teams of Ph.D. students even if society does not want to employ them afterwards. Indeed, a case can be made that in our present social condition the university is more important as a research institute than as a professional school. It employs scientists and scholars who work on the frontiers of the unknown, so it is uniquely equipped with sensitive intellectual antennae to detect coming changes in the social environment and to propose responses to them—in a word, to speed up the homeostatic mechanism. Thus predictions about an energy crisis and strategies for dealing with it or reflections on the future of conurbations or on the equitable distribution of wealth all should be expected to come from faculties of applied science, economics, and sociology. Here is the expertise, the detachment from day-to-day decision-making, the wide horizon of imagination. Indeed, of all contemporary social institutions, universities seem to be the most appropriate to act as the guides to long-term goals and custodians of the future interests of mankind. If this is an appropriate function (and I believe it is), the most needed service of the universities to the community is not the conventional extension work which we associate with the land-grant college philosophy; it is the application of their unique multidisciplinary wisdom to the techniques of adaptation to social change.

This conflict of interest between the university as a purveyor of graduates and the university as a nerve centre for research makes adaptation to social change difficult. But there are more serious difficulties than this. I wrote in the preface that we live at a time of unprecedented crisis. I would now revise that statement, for a crisis is something which passes, something from which one recovers after taking remedial action, something to be overcome by temporary discomforts and sacrifices. What we are now entering is a climacteric of civilisation. We shall *forever* have to concern ourselves with population control, the husbandry of scarce resources, the risk of disruption of cities by malfunctioning of technical equipment or by non-cooperation from minority groups or by murder at the hands of urban guerillas. We shall reach the stage when no one can have more without someone having less. This steady state will exacerbate the tensions of urban living.

We have little experience of how to conduct ourselves in such a society, but clearly the freedom which will matter most will be freedom from envy of one's neighbour. All the rhetoric about the need for a revised scale of values and concern with quality of life rather than with material living standards will have to be translated into political action. Regardless of how this change comes about, we can be sure that the universities will be deeply involved. Why? Not only because of their research expertise, but also because, as we move toward mass higher education, the social values of college graduates will more and more influence the social values of the nation. What the university stands for in public morality will affect what its thousands of graduates stand for.

Universities are poorly equipped for this task. Throughout most of their history they were religious foundations. This led them into bigotry, superstition, and intolerance; but there were precious compensations, for the Christian ethic included a code of principles and the moral courage to live by them: a disregard for superfluous wealth, a disdain for conspicuous consumption, a sense of service to one's fellow men and of the responsibility which goes with privilege. And when dogmatic religion cooled, the Christian ethic remained. This ethic—in nineteenth-century Oxford—was implied by a "gentleman's education." To suggest that universities should still function as finishing schools for gentlemen is to invite ridicule, and the student who has this attitude is an almost extinct species. But before we congratulate ourselves on this purging from the university of an unwanted type, let us remind ourselves that a public morality permeated by qualities like these may be essential if we are going to survive the transition from a world of expansion to a steady-state world. So this is a third challenge to the capacity of universities to adapt themselves to social change, and since secular universities have forgotten their ancient spiritual heritage, it is the most difficult challenge of all.

Universities, then, have their own peculiar and difficult problems of managing their homeostatic response to the environment. If their management is wise they can give a lead to society in indicating the directions of adaptation rather than (as so often in the past) dragging behind. Beyond the suggestions in the preceding chapters, I have no recipes for success in this endeavour; but I can end with one observation from a lifetime of experience: Universities will not respond coherently to the social changes affecting their several functions if they are overadministered, too monolithic in structure, or too hierarchical. This seems to be a paradox but it is not, for a university functions as an inverted hierarchy. The future of the university, the way in which it reconciles tradition and innovation, will be determined less by trustees and presidents than by the values of thousands of individual teachers. Ideas and initiative do not come downwards from the administration as directives to be obeyed; they percolate upwards from individual scholars and scientists as recommendations to be approved by the administration. No other great institution works quite like this. The university must.

References

ASHBY, E. *Community of Universities.* Cambridge: Cambridge University Press, 1963.

ASHBY, E. *Universities: British, Indian, African.* London: Weidenfeld and Nicolson, 1966.

ASHBY, E. *Any Person, Any Study.* New York: McGraw-Hill, 1971.

BAGEHOT, W. *The English Constitution.* London: Collins, 1963.

BARZUN, J. *The American University: How It Runs; Where It Is Going.* New York: Harper and Row, 1968.

BERNAL, J. D. *The Social Function of Science.* London: Routledge and Kegan Paul, 1939.

BERNAL, J. D. "After Twenty-Five Years." In M. Goldsmith (Ed.), *The Science of Science.* London: Souvenir Press, 1964.

BERNAL, J. D. *Science in History.* London: Watts, 1969.

BRUNER, J. "The New Educational Technology." In A. de Grazia and

D. A. Sohn (Eds.), *Revolution in Teaching*. New York: Bantam, 1964.

BUTTERFIELD, H. *The Universities and Education Today*. London: Routledge, 1962.

CARTER, T. F. *The Invention of Printing in China and Its Spread Westward*. New York: Columbia University Press, 1931.

CLARK, B., AND TROW, M. "The Organizational Context" ("Determinants of College Student Subcultures"). In T. M. Newcomb and E. K. Wilson (Eds.), *College Peer Groups: Problems and Prospects for Research*. Chicago: Aldine-Atherton, 1966.

CLOUD, P. (Ed.) *Resources and Man*. San Francisco: Freeman, 1969.

FRYE, N. "The Knowledge of Good and Evil." In M. Black (Ed.), *The Morality of Scholarship*. Ithaca, N.Y.: Cornell University Press, 1967.

GARDNER, J. W. *Excellence*. New York: Harper and Row, 1961.

HARVARD UNIVERSITY. *General Education in a Free Society. Report of the Harvard Committee*. Cambridge, Mass.: Harvard University Press, 1945.

Higher Education: Report of the Committee Appointed by the Prime Minister Under the Chairmanship of Lord Robbins 1961–63. London: H.M.S.O., 1963.

HUXLEY, A. *Science, Liberty and Peace*. London: Chatto and Windus, 1947.

JASPERS, K. *The Idea of the University*. London: Peter Owen, 1960.

KENISTON, K. "Human and Social Benefits." In *Universal Higher Education: Costs, Benefits, Options*. Washington, D.C.: American Council on Education, 1972.

LAPLACE, J. *A Philosophical Essay on Probabilities*. London: Constable, 1951.

MACKAY, D. M. "Machines and Societies." In G. Wolstenholme (Ed.), *Man and His Future*. London: Churchill, 1963.

MARCUSE, H. *One-Dimensional Man*. Boston, Beacon, 1964.

MEADOWS, D. L. *Toward Global Equilibrium: Collected Papers*. Cambridge, Mass.: Wright-Allen, 1973.

MOBERLY, W. *The Crisis in the University*. London: S.C.M. Press, 1949.

MYERS, E. D. *Education in the Perspective of History*. New York: Harper and Row, 1960.

NEWMAN, J. H. *On the Scope and Nature of University Education*. London: J. M. Dent, 1915.

Oriental, East European and African Studies. Hayter Report. London: H.M.S.O., 1961.

PAULSEN, F. *The German Universities and University Study*. London: Longmans Green, 1908.

PIPPARD, A. B. "Outline of a Proposal for Reorganising University Education." In *The Flow into Employment of Scientists, Engineers and Technologists*. Swann Report. London: H.M.S.O., 1968.

PIPPARD, A. B., PARKES, E. W., NICOL, A. D. I., AND DEER, W. A. "University Developments in the 1970s." *Nature, London*, 1970, *228*, 813–815.

POLANYI, M. "The Republic of Science." *Minerva*, 1962, *1*, 59.

PRICE, D. *The Scientific Estate*. Cambridge, Mass.: Harvard University Press, 1965.

RABINOWITCH, E. "The Scientific Revolution." *Bulletin of Atomic Scientists*, Oct.–Dec. 1963.

ROSE, H., AND ROSE, S. *Science and Society*. London: Pelican, 1970.

ROSZAK, T. *The Making of a Counter Culture*. New York: Anchor, 1969.

SCHELER, M. *Die Formen des Wissens und der Bildung*. Bonn, 1925.

SKINNER, B. F. *The Behaviour of Organisms*. New York: Appleton-Century, 1938.

STONE, R. "A Model of the Educational System." *Minerva*, 1965, *3*, 172–186.

STONE, R. "Input, Output and Demagogic Accounting: A Tool for Educational Planning." *Minerva*, 1966, *4*, 365–380.

UNIVERSITY OF CALIFORNIA, BERKELEY, ACADEMIC SENATE. *Education at Berkeley: Report of the Select Committee on Education*. Muscatine Report. Berkeley, 1966.

VEBLEN, T. *The Higher Learning in America*. New York: Sagamore Press, 1957.

VON HUMBOLDT, W. *Schriften zur Politik und zum Bildungswesen*. Darmstadt, 1964.

WEINBERG, A. "But Is the Teacher Also a Citizen." In B. R. Keenan (Ed.), *Science and the University*. New York: Columbia University Press, 1966.

WEINBERG, A. "Social Problems and National Socio-Technical Institutes." In National Academy of Sciences, *Applied Science and Technological Progress: A Report to the Committee on Science and Astronautics, U.S. House of Representatives*. Washington: Government Printing Office, 1967.

WISSENSCHAFTSRAT. *Empfehlungen des Wissenschaftsrats zum Ausbau der Wissenschaftlichen Einrichtungen. Teil I. Wissenschaftliche Hochschule*. Bonn: Bundesdruckerei, 1960.

WISSENSCHAFTSRAT. *Anregungen des Wissenschaftsrates zur Gestalt neuer Hochschulen.* Bonn: Bundesdruckerei, 1962.

WISSENSCHAFTSRAT. *Empfehlungen zur Neuordnung des Studiums an den Wissenshaftlichen Hochschulen.* Bonn: Bundesdruckerei, 1966.

WOODHALL, M., AND BLAUG, M. "Productivity Trends in British University Education." *Minerva,* 1965, *3,* 483–498.

Index

155